Aspects of
Wilde

ALSO AVAILABLE FROM SOLIS PRESS:
BY VINCENT O'SULLIVAN
The Good Girl
A Book of Bargains
Sentiment
Sentiment and Other Stories
Human Affairs
A Dissertation Upon Second Fiddles
The Green Window

OF RELATED INTEREST
Oscar Wilde: A Study by André Gide
Aubrey Beardsley by Arthur Symons
William Thomas Horton: A Selection of His Work by Roger Ingpen

Aspects of Wilde

Vincent O'Sullivan

Solis Press

PUBLISHER'S DEDICATION:
This book is dedicated to DAVID LEPPER M.A. on the occasion of the award of a master of arts degree from Cardiff University.

First published in 1936 by Henry Holt & Company, New York. This edition completely reset with minor spelling changes. A new introduction and a list of people mentioned have been added to this 2025 edition.

Caution: this book contains words and views that are offensive and upsetting. The book was first published in 1936 when such attitudes and language were not challenged.

Published in 2025 by Solis Press

Copyright © 2025 Solis Press
Introduction copyright © 2025 Lesley Gray
Biographical notes copyright © 2025 George Cavendish

All rights reserved. No part of this publication may be reproduced, stored in a retrieval system, or transmitted, in any form or by any means, electronic, mechanical, photocopying, recording or otherwise, except as permitted by the UK Copyright, Designs and Patents Act 1988, without the prior permission of the publisher.

This book is sold subject to the condition that it shall not, by way or trade or otherwise, be lent, resold, hired out or otherwise circulated without the publisher's prior consent in any form of binding or cover other than in which it is published and without a similar condition including this condition being imposed on the subsequent purchaser.

ISBN: 978-1-910146-91-0 (hbk)
ISBN: 978-1-910146-93-4 (pbk)

Published by Solis Press, England

Web: www.solispress.com | *X/Twitter*: @SolisPress

Contents

Bernard Shaw's opinion	vi
Publisher's note to the 2025 edition	vii
From the 1936 cover	vii
Introduction to the 2025 edition	ix
Introductory	1
Chapter I	3
Chapter II	14
Chapter III	16
Chapter IV	22
Chapter V	27
Chapter VI	52
Chapter VII	61
Chapter VIII	78
Chapter IX	86
Chapter X	92
Chapter XI	102
Chapter XII	110
Chapter XIII	114
Chapter XIV	119
Epilogue	129
Biographical notes	133

Bernard Shaw's opinion

"These reminiscences of Mr. Vincent O'Sullivan's should be published if only to clean up the superfluous mud that has been heaped on the story of Oscar Wilde's last days in Paris.

"Mr. O'Sullivan, an authentic personal acquaintance of Wilde in those days, with no special affection for him nor any reason for whitewashing him, gives the first sane and credible description of him.

"Mr. O'Sullivan testifies that Oscar was not unpresentable, not unclean, not drunk and incapable in the police court sense, and that he remained to the last the best company in the world, as he had always been. He talked to the end; and Mr. O'Sullivan makes the very interesting observation that as talking was Oscar Wilde's appointed work in this world, with him talking to the end meant working to the end. Unfortunately he tried the too common experiment of working on a diet of alcohol, like Edmund Kean, Robson, and other brilliant actors; and this meant premature death; but it did not mean being drunk and disorderly, or dirty, or ill dressed.

"His last recorded words 'I am dying as I have lived, beyond my means,' proclaimed an undaunted and, Wildeanly speaking, an edifying end; and Mr. O'Sullivan has done a service to literary history by restoring the true tone of that particular chapter of it."

Publisher's note to the 2025 edition

This revised edition for 2025 includes a specially written introduction by Lesley Gray, Ph.D. in Comparative Literature.

As this book contains many, many names, some of which may not be familiar to the reader, the publisher has included biographical notes at the end of the book with a brief description. The assistance of George Cavendish in preparing this list is gratefully acknowledged.

From the 1936 cover

This generous, authentic and knowledgeable book is designed, in its author's own words, "to lift Wilde out of the miasmas which still float round his name and place him frankly and clearly where he ought to be: in the history of English literature." Mr. O'Sullivan, who was born in New York but has lived most of his life in England and France, knew Wilde well, but not so well as to feel under any obligation to his memory to tell anything but the truth about him. His estimate of Wilde and Wilde's work, therefore, is neither biased nor vindictive. He has succeeded in producing a fascinating blend of personal anecdote, literary criticism and vindication without hero worship, the whole finely flavoured with the taste of the period of the unhappy man's rise and fall. There are also interesting sidelights on many of Wilde's contemporaries, both English and French—Dowson, Pater, Beardsley, Smithers, George Moore, Gide, Zola and others.

Introduction to the 2025 edition

WHILE THERE HAVE BEEN many biographies of the famous writer, playwright and poet, *Aspects of Wilde* offers a series of intimate portraits of Oscar Wilde's later life as witnessed by the Irish-American writer Vincent O'Sullivan, a man some 14 years Wilde's junior. Although O'Sullivan had first encountered Wilde as a celebrated member of the literary circles of late nineteenth-century London, and Wilde had read some of O'Sullivan's work, it was only when Wilde fled to Europe after his release from Reading gaol that O'Sullivan got to know him well. In fact, O'Sullivan became a something of a benefactor to the now broken and impoverished Wilde, standing by him while many kept their distance as they were fearful of being tainted by association with Wilde's tattered reputation.

Aspects of Wilde was written over 30 years after the death of Wilde, when O'Sullivan himself was in the latter stages of his life. It has to be said that there is a degree of rambling and repetition in the text, but despite this, the insights offered into the life and personality of Wilde, as well as a consideration of Wilde's place among other figures of literature and art, are so rich in the telling that any faults can perhaps be forgiven. As part recollection, part literary commentary of Wilde, O'Sullivan offers an unusual and intelligent perspective of this great literary figure that is both poignant and honest. As George Bernard Shaw, a contemporary of Wilde and a fellow Irishman, noted in his 'Opinion', included on page vi of this book, O'Sullivan's work "gives the first sane and credible description of him [Wilde], … and clean[s] up the superfluous mud that has been heaped upon the story of Oscar Wilde's last days in Paris".

Coming from a rich family, Vincent O'Sullivan was untroubled by financial worries and free to pursue his literary interests and ambitions. Based in London in the 1890s, he was noticed by Leonard Smithers, a publisher notorious for his risqué output and close association with the artists and writers who became known as the Decadents, a movement that challenged and defied conventional societal norms by focusing on sensual excess rather than the moral structure which was more usual in the reading material of the time. O'Sullivan with his penchant for Gothic morbidity, somewhat reminiscent of Poe, became part of "Smither's people", a group that included the artist Aubrey Beardsley, writer Ernest Dowson and poet Arthur Symons.

After Wilde's release from prison, Smithers came forward to offer his services as publisher to Wilde on forthcoming works. Eventually, in 1898, Smithers released the now famous *Ballad of Reading Gaol*, which was received with great acclaim, despite the true author's identity being concealed from readers or some time. According to O'Sullivan, Smithers claimed that "I'll publish anything that the others are afraid of" (page 63). This was certainly true of *The Ballad of Reading Gaol*, as no-one else would risk taking on the work of a man who was now a social outcast.

As Wilde became part of Smither's French circle so O'Sullivan, who had moved to France, came to know him well. Wilde had commented on O'Sullivan's work, writing in a letter to Smithers about *The Houses of Sin* (1897), that these poems were "more concentrated in motive … more fully realized" than O'Sullivan's earlier works that Wilde must have read, adding "but in what a midnight his soul seems to walk" (O'Sullivan's *Opinions*, with an introduction by Alan Anderson, p. 9, 1959). On the man himself, Wilde reported to Robert Ross from Paris in 1890, "I dined with Vincent O'Sullivan last night; he was really rather pleasant, for one who treats life from the standpoint of the tomb" (from Alan Anderson, p. 9).

O'Sullivan categorically states that Wilde was not a close friend, nonetheless they met often and O'Sullivan seems to have become inveigled in Wilde's complicated affairs, encountering him not only in France but also when Wilde travelled to Italy with Lord Alfred Douglas. Indeed, when Douglas was ordered back to England by his mother, leaving Wilde alone and penniless, it was O'Sullivan who came to his rescue.

These philanthropic encounters did not stop O'Sullivan from maintaining an objective view of Wilde and his work. It is from this time that O'Sullivan was able to construct a vivid and at times critical appraisal of Wilde. Using his wide knowledge both of literature as well as prominent social and artistic figures, O'Sullivan offers a colourful and unique picture of both the man and his work, providing a valuable addition to Wilde scholarship.

O'Sullivan writes much on Wilde's need to entertain, commenting that his great fear was to bore. This was particularly evident in Wilde's plays, with O'Sullivan noting that "the written version was often inferior to the spoken" (page 101). O'Sullivan maintained that Wilde was more of an orator than a playwright. He recalls the struggle that Wilde had to commit the words of *Salome* to paper. Wilde's skills as an accomplished speaker suggested to O'Sullivan that these would have made Wilde an excellent candidate for politics, commenting that the playwright Sheridan shared such a talent.

In a final irony, O'Sullivan's own financial demise resulted in him falling ill and becoming destitute in France. This man who had been so generous to Wilde in his hour of need now himself relied upon the kindness of others. Those who helped O'Sullivan included Lord Alfred Douglas, Natalie Clifford Barney, an American woman writer who had met Wilde when she was a child (and later had relationships with Dolly Wilde, Wilde's niece), as well as Olive Custance, who married Lord Alfred Douglas.

O'Sullivan died in July 1940 in the pauper ward of the Hôpital Saint-Antoine in Paris. No one came forward to claim O'Sullivan's body and eventually his bones were housed in an ossuary in the Parisian suburb of Thiais. But his work lives on, not least in *Aspects of Wilde* which was his attempt to "lift him [Wilde] out of the miasma … [and into the] history of the English literature" (page 2).

Vincent O'Sullivan

In this book, the influences on Wilde, such as Pater, Ruskin and Huygens, his admiration for the women he encountered such as Lily Langtry and Sarah Bernhardt, as well as his loyal friends, most notably Robbie Ross, are examined. In addition, Wilde's generosity and lack of rancour are particularly evident in the recollections. As well as amusing anecdotes, O'Sullivan does not shy away from the pathos of Wilde's later years. He also gives insights into Wilde's friendships and enemies, of which there were many, although the former dwindled somewhat during his final years.

A comprehensive list of names of all those mentioned in the text, together with short biographical details is provided in the final section of the book to give contextual guidance.

Lesley Gray, PhD in Comparative Literature

Introductory

THE OBJECT OF THE following pages is to place an historical figure in an historical position. There is an enduring interest in Wilde; whatever the value of his work, he is not forgotten. Four books on the subject appeared in one year (1929–1930) in France alone.[1] His writings have been translated into the chief European languages and into some minor languages also.

The title I have placed on the title-page gives the explanation of this book. I knew Wilde pretty well. I was never under the slightest obligation to him. I have no grievance against him either. Therefore what I have written may be taken as being without bias of any kind. I have not tried to surprise one who put his genius into his life in situations unworthy of his genius. The spirit guiding what is here written is well enough indicated by the words which De Quincey found himself obliged to add to his recollections of Coleridge: "I must inform the reader that I was not, nor ever had been, the friend of Coleridge in any sense which could have the right to restrain my frankest opinions upon his merits. I never had lived in such intercourse with Coleridge as to give me the opportunity of becoming his friend. To *him* I owed nothing at all."

The memory of this illustrious man tends to be the prey, on the one hand, of the mythical biographer, ill-informed and sensational at all costs, and on the other, of the prurient and vulgar-minded—people who think there is something vaguely indecent

---

[1] Two by Davray and Vernon. The others were by Charles Grolleau, the Catholic writer, and Madame Lucie Delarue-Mardrus. There were perhaps others still which I have not seen. Léon Lemonnier's Biography was published in 1932. Studies of Wilde in other European countries are too numerous to mention. Several translations of English books have also been published and are appearing up to the date of writing. To all these should be added M. Maurice Rostand's play which ran for several months in Paris during 1935.

in all that concerns him. I would lift him out of the miasmas which still float round his name and place him frankly and clearly where he ought to be: in the history of English Literature.

I have been obliged to use the first personal pronoun more than I like. Readers will excuse me: they will see that this was inevitable, given the plan of the book and the way it is composed.

[Vincent O'Sullivan]
Prague, 1932.
Fontarabia, 1935.

I

About ten years after the last war a letter appeared in a London newspaper from a correspondent who had been visiting Père-Lachaise, the vast burial ground in Paris. As he strolled, he came upon a guardian and asked him what graves among those of so many renowned people he was oftenest asked to shew. The guardian mentioned the names of Alfred de Musset, Chopin, some others, and then added: "But for once I am asked for any other grave here, I am asked ten times to point out the grave of Oscar Wilde."

So that strange career seems to continue as if by magic in an after-life hardly more explicable than the first.

Magic, a sorcery emanating from the spirit, was long held to be the explanation of the equally astonishing career—a career in many respects like Oscar Wilde's—of Apuleius in the second century.[2] Here was one who charmed the world by his wit, artful speech, and the pomp of his demeanour. His lectures were thronged by admirers, and the curious, and his enemies. All subjects came well to this master of language, from speculations on human destiny to the minor social arts. He brought the philosophy of Plato and other subtle matters to the comprehension of fashionable society in Carthage. He was dragged through the law-courts in a trial of a scandalous character, and eventually had a great fame, not explained by the value of his writings, which spread far beyond his native Africa to Rome, to Greece, and wherever there was civilization.

As there were perhaps better writers in the Africa of Apuleius who had not his renown and are lost to us, so were there certainly

---

[2] Some of the writings of Apuleius are not unlike Wilde's—the third Chapter of *Florida*, for instance. The last sentence is quite in the manner of Wilde; it might pass for his.

in the England of Wilde; but their graves no man or woman seeks to know. They could not cast the magic spell. To speak for myself, I have never cared much for Wilde's writings taken as a collection. What I do care for among them, his *Fairy Tales* and *The Sphynx*, are neglected by most of his admirers. He himself did not rate these things among his best work, though he gave them their value, for he considered all he wrote important. And, in a restricted sense, it is.

He told me that one day, Beerbohm Tree, the actor, came to see him, and found him looking through the script of *A Woman of No Importance*, which Tree was to produce. Tree asked him what he was doing. "I am making some slight changes in the text," replied Wilde. "But after all, who am I to tamper with a masterpiece?"

Of course he meant this to be taken humorously both by Tree to whom he said it and by me to whom he told it. Still, it expressed his conviction. He did think that *A Woman of No Importance* and his other plays were masterpieces. If a man's power of feeling confidence in himself and in the value of his acts be a benefit, Wilde was generously dowered by nature.

"Praise makes me humble," he said to me another time. "But when I am abused I know I have touched the stars."

* * *

Walter Pater, he thought, was far too sensitive to the criticisms of people not fit to tie his shoes. Once at Oxford he came on Pater brooding over an article which attempted to turn into ridicule his essay on Charles Lamb. The article was entitled: "Lamb—and Mint Sauce," and was written, according to Wilde, by H. D. Traill, a writer of considerable repute.

Wilde was dumbfounded. He said his estimation of Pater as a man altered from that moment. "Just imagine! Pater! I could not conceive how one could be Pater and yet be susceptible to the insults of the lowest kind of journalism."

In that is all the difference between Pater and the vulgarizer of Pater. Wilde was much more than that, but he was that too. He always professed a great admiration for Pater's books. For the man he seemed to have the slightly contemptuous pity of one who lives in the sight of the public, despises it, and dominates it easily, for another who dreads the public and is morbidly sensitive to its hostility. From Pater I took the impression that he was not enthusiastic about Wilde and his writings. He said something very severe about "Mr. Wilde," as he called him, which I prefer to leave in darkness. His notice of *Dorian Gray* is a remarkable example of dexterity, for the book must have scandalized him in many ways. He, too, seemed to prefer Wilde's *Fairy Tales* to the rest of his production.

* * *

But Wilde was not at all pleased if one praised his *Fairy Tales* at the expense of the rest of his work. I believe he thought his plays the most important things he had done. The plays, with the exception of *The Importance of Being Earnest* and *Salome*, derive very definitely from a French school long out of fashion, represented by Scribe, Augier, George Sand, the second Dumas, and Sardou. The substance is melodramatic. What saves them, what makes them viable, what casts a glamour over them, is the style and the wit which, say what they will, was Wilde's very own, not only different from what any of his contemporaries produced, but different from what any one at any time in the history of literature has produced. In his peculiar form of wit, Wilde had imitators, but no predecessors.

Sometimes Whistler's wit is compared to Wilde's. It was quite something else. Whistler was malignant. Whistler's wit was like the prongs of a rake which, dragged across the subject of it, left a poisonous wound, as it was meant to do. Wilde's is full of tolerance and good-humour and high spirits, as the man was himself. It is not meant to be a stab, but a cocktail.

With that, and his sense of dramatic situation, and a shallow, not altogether original, but very clear and consistent philosophy, easily grasped, his plays make a good show, and it is not surprising that they are now played in various languages, while those of Dumas, which have dramatic situation and wit, and also a preaching philosophy, but no tolerance and good-humour, are not played out of France, and not much in it, and those of Scribe, which have only dramatic situation, are not played anywhere. As with the two others, as with Pinero who belongs to the same school, Wilde's dramatic situations may be called artificial. In life, we say, things don't happen so neatly as that. Still, the moment we touch the theatre we touch convention. In all plays is the element of make-believe: that is what the spectators are there for. A plain photographic and stenographic report of life would be unbearable on the stage. And life does really offer dramatic situations—too many of them. Even Tchekov, the master of writing in minors, who does his best to be drab, has to fall back on the revolver shot.

The best stage-play writers at present do no more attempt to get rid of the dramatic situation than did Sardou or Wilde. What they try for is to go round it and to treat it quietly. In the hands of a very modern French or German dramatist, "Mrs. Arbuthnot" would not hit her ex-lover across the face with a glove. But she would show that she had it in her to do it, or something equivalent more cerebrally cruel. Which is closer to life it were hard to decide. Perhaps both. But, as was said, it is not the business of the drama to deal with life as it is lived. Do that and you bore your public; and a play that does not please a large public does not exist as a play. On the stage the incessant calamity of the times can only be shown in samples more abrupt, more immediate, than reality.

In a theatre Wilde's plays are found interesting by those who are there not for an evening's instruction, or an evening's shock, or an evening's patriotism, or for anything else than an evening's entertainment. I read some of them again not long ago and found, rather to my surprise, that they were pleasant to read. Once the theatricalism is accepted, the nimble intelligence, the surprising wit, the general good form, carry the acts happily along. And in his plays, at any rate, it cannot be said of Wilde, *sufflaminandus erat*. For a man so enveloped in words, who wrote so easily, who had such huge battalions of phrases at command, he shows a noteworthy restraint. He wanders far less away from the business in hand than any of the Russians except Gogol; less than Strindberg too, or Bernard Shaw. This is due to the fact that when he sat down to write, his intention was simply to make a play, and not to preach, or to enforce a doctrine, or to explode against social wrongs, or to right wrongs in the wrong way. I once read that *A Woman of No Importance* was a powerful accusation of the treatment meted out to the unmarried mother; but that surely is to lean too heavily on a dramatic situation which had the run of the streets long before Wilde's time.

In reality Wilde has only a small number of ideas in his plays and they are very simple. He disliked hypocrisy in social intercourse, he glorified individualism, he denied the moral right of the community to sacrifice the life of any member of it. These ideas he hardly ever expressed directly like Dumas *fils* and Augier. He was either more afraid of his audiences, or he had not the same confidence in their patience if they were preached at. When the American girl in *A Woman of No Importance* gives what seems to be a sincere deliverance of what Wilde really thought, he cuts short the tirade with a joke, and, seeming to mock his own sincerity, he nullifies the effect of it. He resigned himself to be the amuser from fear of being the bore. In this he was wrong; he wronged himself, and he deprived his plays of a permanent element. For just at that time the drama of ideas was coming into vogue in

England, and Wilde lost the chance of being a pioneer. He left it to Bernard Shaw, and to Archer with his translations from Ibsen. He was satisfied with scattering not so much ideas as notions of ideas amid the witty and amusing dialogue, and they appear in fragments, in the course of a reply, not causing the least delay in the exposure of the anecdote, not detaching attention from the plot. Besides, the characters as conceived are not vehicles for ideas, not even in the play where he allows himself to think.

* * *

To be an effective criticism of the unmarried mother's lot, the characters in *A Woman of No Importance* would have to be real characters, built and rounded from the feet up and moving in their own special atmosphere. Now that is just what the characters are not in any of Wilde's plays. It has been said that between him and Sheridan the English drama is a desolation, and some admirers have put him on a level with Sheridan. I don't think Wilde was as great a man from any point of view as Sheridan; as a dramatist he was certainly not so good. "Bob Acres," "Mrs. Malaprop," the "Teazles," "Sir Lucius O'Trigger," and even "Lydia Languish" are real characters: we can continue their lives, we can guess what they are likely to do when they are out of sight and hearing. But how can one continue the lives of figures made all of a piece, like "Lord Illingworth" and "Mrs. Allonby"? In Wilde's theatre there are two kinds of characters, and only two. There are the discs which give forth their Master's voice: such are "Illingworth," "Mrs. Allonby," and others. And then there are theatrical conventions, phantoms arising from the dust of the stage of pretty much the same substance and quality as may be found in the arid reaches of the British drama stretching between Sheridan and Wilde. Two plays of Bulwer-Lytton, *Money* and *The Lady of Lyons*, create the same atmosphere as Wilde's plays and develop at the same pitch. Wilde may have eked these figures out with some rags taken from Scribe, and George Sand, and Dumas, and even Augier and Sardou; but most of the British dramatists of the nineteenth century who came before Wilde had gone to the same models. He did it a little better, that's all. But Wilde could not make figures like "Gerald Arbuthnot" and his mother, and "Lady Windermere," and others, anything but stuffed figures. Agitated by false passions, moving in false situations, how could they seem genuine? But he had the advantage over Sheridan, and of course over the Robertsons, Tom Taylors, even over Lytton, of being a real poet, and accordingly he is sometimes seized by his own characters and pauses to watch them live like human beings. "Mrs. Erlynne" is one I recall just now.

* * *

It would appear that he considered the actress who first played this part [Mrs. Erlynne], Miss Marion Terry, as the most satisfactory of all those, men or women, who appeared in his plays. But the part is the best in his repertory. Often, his view and the player's view did not agree. The players did not always take his observations in good part. He told me that one day he remarked to the actor, Terry [most probably Fred Terry], who was rehearsing the part of "Gerald Arbuthnot" in *A Woman of No Importance*, that he wished him to be light and boyish, whereas Terry was representing the character as a hardened man of the world.

"Oh, well, you know, Mr. Wilde," said Terry curtly, "you can lead a horse to the water, but you can't make him drink."

"No, Terry," replied Wilde. "But you have a circus. In that circus is a ring. A horse enters the ring and approaches a trough of water. The ring-master cracks his whip and says, 'Drink!' and the horse drinks. That horse, Terry, is the actor."

Terry was furious, said Wilde. "So, Mr. Wilde, you compare the stage to a circus?"

"Ah," said Wilde blandly, "yours was the metaphor."

Vincent O'Sullivan

***

Wilde's plays cannot be taken as an image of life, or even of the life of his time. There is no hint of the pressure of the fatal ring. George Gissing was a contemporary of Wilde; but the England he presents in his novels and the England Wilde reflects in his plays might lie a thousand years apart. Wilde disliked realism in art and in life. Even after his imprisonment, I think he still saw the world through a romantic haze, which, after all, gives a result as ultimately true as seeing it through a realistic haze. Zola he abhorred with some respect, and George Moore he abhorred with some contempt. Nobody could be much in his company without learning his opinion of George Moore, and that is why I mention it here.

"Have you read *Evelyn Innes*?" I asked him.

"I hear it has to be played on the piano," he answered.[3]

He told me more than once, and perhaps he has written it somewhere, that dialect should be only indicated: an attempt to reproduce it exactly was bad art. How true this is may be realized by anyone who looks, for instance, at George Eliot's vinegar "Mrs. Poyser," once considered a comic character, or at a number of American tales and novels, or Cockney tales. Nothing in the vast world of writing is more afflicting.

But Wilde, however resolved he was not to portray the sad or the ugly, still less the squalid, might have let a little more of the sounds of the life of the last years of the nineteenth century into his elegant boudoirs and drawing-rooms. He does it no more than the W. S. Gilberts, the Wills, the Tom Taylors, and the best of them, Lytton, who preceded him.

---

[3] As this book, *Evelyn Innes*, may be unknown to the present generation of novel readers, it is well to add that it had to do with operas and the amours of opera-singers.

Now Sheridan, with whom he is so often compared, though he dealt with people of the same social rating as Wilde did, manages to open some outlooks on the rough general life of the eighteenth century. They are not many, but they are enough to save his plays from being just theatrical productions without application elsewhere. For no matter how rich or how highly placed in the social scale people may be, they are bound to be affected in some way or other by the rough general life of their time; and that was still more true of the last half of the nineteenth century in England than of the last half of the eighteenth. That the lives of manual workers must be necessarily more interesting than the lives of the opulent class is a fallacy; and what has been said need not be taken as a regret that Wilde kept to the opulent class—which was indeed the only class he knew much about.

But it is to be taken as a regret that more of his stage-figures are not embodied in flesh instead of in paste and paint. 'Tis only the eye of childhood that takes seriously a painted devil. Till his own tragedy overcame him, Wilde made no attempt to come to close quarters with the bitter aspects of life: "Dorian Gray" is not a tragic figure. The test of the tragic figure is that it rouses a feeling of pity in the right-minded; but one feels no more pity for "Dorian Gray" than for the Sadics and maniacs invented by Edgar Allan Poe.

After his downfall, Wilde did make an attempt to get on terms with his own tragedy. He wrote *De Profundis*. He also wrote the *Ballad [of Reading Gaol]*, which, if it be not good poetry, is at least a recital full of anguish. Whether he would have developed in this new direction if he had continued to write, no one can say. Personally, I do not think so. He told me very elaborately the plans of two plays which he thought of writing. They were both taken from the Bible—the story of Pharaoh and the captive Jews, and the story of Queen Jezebel. They were both impressive as he related them, and would doubtless have had great success if he had written them. But they were both in his old manner—the manner of *Salome*.

* * *

One might go a step farther. On Wilde his tragedy had a physical effect resulting in a dissolution of that will-power which enabled him to overcome his natural indolence and to turn his thoughts, not only into spoken but into written words. Discouragement sat heavy on his shoulders; the French words, *à quoi bon?* became his daily anthem. But his essential attitude to life had not changed. As this was when he came from Oxford in the eighteen-eighties and captured London, so it remained to the end. On most men, such a catastrophe as his, set about with so many circumstances of injustice and needless humiliation, would have had a corroding and ruinous action, or else an action prompted by hate and vengeance. But Wilde did not seem to harbour any grudge against society. He had not become an anarchist. His loyalty to England was unchanged, and also his admiration for Queen Victoria, who was one of his heroines. Only a year or so before his death he said to me:

"The three women I have most admired are Queen Victoria, Sarah Bernhardt, and Lily Langtry. I would have married any one of them with pleasure," he added, laughing.

At the time of the Boer War he was not pro-Boer, but pro-English. Anti-English feeling, always latent in France, ran high there at that time, especially in Paris; but Wilde did not share it. I witnessed a discussion between him and a French journalist on this subject. The Frenchman fiercely denounced the brutality and tyranny of the English in general, and in particular as shewn by their invasion of a peace-loving pastoral country-side. He was utterly astonished to find Wilde defending the English side of the case. He considered it one of Wilde's paradoxes and insincerities.

"The English prisons must be comfortable," he said venomously, when Wilde was out of earshot.

But Wilde was sincere. Dostoevsky, who suffered a much worse passion at the hands of the Tsar's government, remained loyal to the Tsar, and became a defender of his prerogatives. Dostoevsky had forged a mystical explanation of his sufferings. Wilde had done the same thing. In the thought of both, the State with its judicial apparatus was but a blind machine, like a motor car which runs over the just and the unjust. It was harder for Dostoevsky to come round to this point than for Wilde, for he was naturally as rancorous as Wilde was good-natured. In Wilde there was a good deal of what Cardinal Newman gives as one of the attributes of the "gentleman." He was "too indolent to bear malice."

II

WHEN IT WAS SAID a few pages back that Sheridan was a greater man than Wilde, this regarded the very restricted nature of Wilde's interests. His interests were restricted to art, and to an art from which all the ugly and sorrowful happenings of life are excluded, as much as they are, say, from Rossetti's art. Just here it is not so much a question of his plays, which are artificial, though they indicate his scheme, but of his essays in which his aesthetic philosophy is formulated.

This would not be surprising if he had been a secluded writer like Pater; but he was a man who lived to the full, who liked to be in the torrent of life, and was unhappy if he was alone for long. Now Sheridan, who had most of Wilde's social gifts, and a certain literary gift, had all the other interests of a man who takes a considerable part in the government of a great nation, and that response to all the coarse sides of human nature which we must suppose in one who is in the midst of the rough and tumble of party-politics. And then, if Wilde lived to the full, it was on a much narrower plane than Sheridan. Sheridan, as politician, gambler, man of society, theatre-manager, was ready and willing to keep company with all sorts and conditions of men and women. Wilde only saw much of certain chosen people.

It is because of this width of interest that Sheridan seems a greater man than Wilde.

W. B. Yeats said to me that he thought Wilde was meant for a man of action. I told Wilde this at Naples. He thought it over and observed: "It is interesting to hear Yeats' opinion about one," and then gave a disparaging picture of English political life. Balfour, whom he placed very high in his esteem, had told him that he was often depressed at a political meeting by the thought that he could always bring down the house by simply exclaiming: "After all, gentlemen, you know—Rule, Britannia!"

If Wilde had felt in himself the power to make a career like Sheridan's he would surely have attempted it, for at starting he had rather more in his favour than Sheridan to make such a career easy. Perhaps he was born out of due time for that. Politics in England was a pleasanter business for the fastidious at the end of the eighteenth century than at the end of the nineteenth. Horace Walpole, more dainty than Wilde, was very comfortable in his pocket-borough.

The great difference between Sheridan and Wilde is that Wilde was a poet and Sheridan was not. Wilde has the better of Sheridan in posthumous fame. Sheridan wrote a few plays before he was thirty; for the rest of his life he was a politician. His plays may have great merit, but they have never made any appeal outside the English-language countries. His long political speeches are now too dreary to read. Outside the British Isles his is a practically unknown name.

Oscar Wilde's name is known all over the world, and his books are current in many languages. Sheridan was no doubt the greater man. Still, a poet and writer is also in his way a man of action, but his action develops inwardly before revealing its result in book or play. He himself is the sole witness of his struggles with ideas and words and phantoms; whereas anybody can watch the struggles of a politician. In the particular case of Wilde, it may be said that he was a man of action, even in the usual sense, much more than a vast number who pass for such, for none can deny his influence in certain ways on his time.

III

It is not intended here to write a "Life" of Oscar Wilde. The design is to report such sayings of his as illustrate a commentary on the life and works of a man in whom a number of people in every country where books are known take considerable interest. It is certainly desirable that a general glance, however cursory, should be thrown over the intellectual claims of Oscar Wilde, and an attempt made to isolate the elements which went to the making of such a man.

* * *

He had great admiration for Gustave Flaubert, not the Flaubert of *Madame Bovary*, but of *Salammbô* and *Trois Contes*. Certain of his writings are coloured in the Flaubertian manner. One day, talking of Flaubert, he said: "What I can't understand is how such a man could sit down to work on the same book regularly for hours, day after day, during a year, or two or three years. Now, when I start a thing I must write desperately day and night till it is finished. Otherwise I should lose interest in it, and the first 'bus passing in the street would distract me from it."

He went on to relate how he came to write *Salome*. He had been thinking of this play for some weeks. One day, when he was in Paris, he lunched with some young writers, and he told them his play, inventing and filling in as he talked. This was generally his method. He invented, not in silence, but in talking. Possibly he had inherited the soul of some far away bard who invented his chants as he sang them. The young Frenchmen, among them André Gide, were much impressed by *Salome*.

Wilde returned to his lodgings in the Boulevard des Capucines. He was alone. It was rather late in the afternoon. A blank book was lying on the table and it occurred to him that he might as well write down what he had just been telling. "If the blank book had not been there on the table I should never have dreamed of doing it. I should not have sent out to buy one."

He wrote and wrote. Finally he looked at the clock. It was between ten and eleven at night. "I can't go on like this," he thought. "I must really get something to eat."

At that time, the Grand Café was on the corner of the Boulevard des Capucines and the Rue Scribe. Wilde took his hat and went over there.

"That fellow Rigo [sic] who ran away with the Princesse de Chimay, Clara Ward, was then the leader of the orchestra of Tziganes in the Grand Café. I called him over to my table and said to him: 'I am writing a play about a woman dancing with her bare feet in the blood of a man she has craved for and slain. I want you to play something in harmony with my thoughts.' And Rigo played such wild and terrible music that those who were there ceased their talk and looked at each other with blanched faces. Then I went back and finished *Salome*."

So he said. I don't see why it should not be essentially true. A rather wide and lengthy knowledge of Parisian restaurants leads me to doubt whether the customers at supper, even before the Great War, would be so profoundly affected by music. The detail about the "blanched faces" sounds very Oscar Wilde. But the rest corresponds with what one knows of his habits.

* * *

At any rate, why the story is given here is to lift out of it the Blank Book. If the book had not been there before him on the table he would not have written. If he did not work headlong while the mood was on him, the least thing would distract him from the work. This shews that the impulse to write was never very strong in Wilde. The impulse to compose—yes. But that he satisfied by talking. Afterwards, to reduce his talk to writing must have seemed to him a huge bore and needed a considerable output of will-power. There were so many other things which he might have been doing and would have preferred to do. The representative Writer, the Author, is a man like Flaubert, who cloisters himself for a good part of the year, who prefers writing to anything else, and sacrifices willingly all the pleasures of the many-coloured earth to his writing. Wilde would sacrifice his writing for an invitation to dinner. If he had been a little bourgeois, afraid of his shadow, content like Zola to stay in one room in his slippers, he might have been a really great writer. Or again, a man like Arnold Bennett, who saw as much of various life as Wilde, but did not waste his time, and reduced all he saw to writing without effort, as if by instinct.

But for Wilde writing was not work but inspiration, and so it was not very hard to break utterly such impulse to write as he had. He had not much left when he came out of prison. It soon died down to the socket. Perhaps if Sarah Bernhardt had shown unequivocally that she was willing to produce a play of his, if he would write it, she might have fanned the guttering flame into life. Her refusal to do this, the way she blew hot and cold according to the varying counsels of her friends, left him discouraged. It is painful to think of the life of a man's soul depending thus on inferior persons; but it happens often enough. Wilde saw no outlook. "I have had my hand on the moon," he said to me. "What is the use of trying to rise a little way from the ground?"

Robert Ross was right, I think, when he said that what killed Wilde was that he saw nothing ahead—no future worth living for. He himself told me that three or four years before his imprisonment he had his palm read by a fortune-teller. The fortune-teller told him quite correctly some events of his past, and then added: "I see a very brilliant life for you up to a certain point. Then I see a wall. Beyond the wall I see nothing."

Another time he said to me: "When I was a boy my two favourite characters were Lucien de Rubempré and Julien Sorel. Lucien hanged himself, Julien died on the scaffold, and I died in prison."

* * *

Somebody to whom I repeated this observed: "Ah, but he didn't," meaning that it were better if he had. Well, the power of acting on a great number of people, his writing power, died in prison. That hope which engenders in a man, even after ostensible disasters, the courage to go on living, died there.

In other respects his faculties seemed unharmed. Those who knew him before and after agree that his talk was as good as ever, and even better, because more easily turned to serious topics, more profound. Here he excelled. He was certainly the best talker of his time, and it is hard to believe that there was ever a better at any time. He had all the gifts necessary: an imposing presence, a pleasant voice, a control of language, charm, and an extraordinary tact in choosing subjects which would suit his listeners, and in judging his effects. What De Quincey says excellently of Coleridge as a talker—"In this lay Coleridge's characteristic advantage, that he was a great natural power, and also a great artist"—may in all truth be said of Wilde. But De Quincey says also that Coleridge reduced his hearers to a flaccid state; and it seems plain that Coleridge's talk was a sort of monologue or lecture on a subject chosen without much regard for those about him. And nobody has said that Coleridge had a sense of humour. Coleridge's talk was evidently more of a performance than Wilde's. He had to get started; he was not always in the mood. But Wilde was spontaneous, no matter what hour of the day or night. He did not try to enforce his moods; he gave the impression of adapting himself to the moods of others.

Probably much nearer to Wilde's talk than Coleridge's was the talk of Villiers de l'Isle-Adam, another Celt. It appears that he too composed his books and plays in talking, and much preferred to talk than to write. But he had not Wilde's physical prestige, his "great natural power"; and they say he often failed to command attention, and that then his listeners got up and went away and left him talking to himself. A greater writer sometimes than Wilde, more indisputably a genius, Villiers had not the elements of popular success that Wilde had in his writings and conversation.

To end on this subject, I will say that there was one side of Wilde's talk which I did not admire. It was a kind of talk he gave to people he did not know very well and wished for some reason or other to fascinate. It was overdone, loaded with crushing compliments, almost oily. Almost? Whenever I heard him going on like that I used to think of Mr. Turveydrop, Dickens's Professor of Deportment. Wilde often used this kind of talk with women. They seemed to like it. Perhaps it was a variation of his national "blarney."

At first, I was disposed to think that sort of thing a practice of irony. Not at all. He had an unequalled command of the comic, and could turn people into ridicule in a way which was seldom cruel or ill-natured, but which, when exercised on certain individuals, did sometimes become ferocious. But there was little irony in his composition, and he did not consider his own life, or the lives of those he knew, or human life in general, ironically.

A corresponding weakness was his mania for correcting the pronunciation and behaviour of those he considered his inferiors in the social order. Sometimes he was right in these lessons in deportment, but he was often wrong, as when one day a true Cockney, accent and all, speaking of Beaumont Street in London, pronounced it *Bewmont*, whereupon Oscar called him to order and in a very lofty tone declared that the correct pronunciation "among people of my class" was Beaumont, as the French would say the word. Sometimes he had right on his side, but a man of sounder manners would doubtless have kept his observations to himself instead of humiliating some victim who had no chance against him. For when the company was numerous, most of those who composed it—considering Oscar as a man who had passed a large part of his time in the company of dukes and princesses, and never questioning his claim (put forward with an authority which the most audacious would be slow to affront) to have issued himself from the highest regions of society—were sure he was infallible in matters of social decorum.

One day he thought fit to correct a young Frenchman—almost a boy—because of the way he ate oysters. He did it in a more acceptable manner than he often shewed in such lessons, but the boy was very much hurt—his meal was spoiled. Oscar made some advances with indolent good-nature and disdain to smooth the matter over. When he had taken himself off, and the others with him, the boy, almost in tears, explained to two of us who remained that his mother had taught him to eat oysters in the way he did. *Ma mère n'est pas princesse, c'est entendu, mais elle a du monde.* We tried to assure him that his mother was right and Wilde wrong—which was indeed the case; but he would not be comforted. So great was the prestige of Wilde upon the young with whom he came in contact, even if they knew hardly anything of what he had written.

IV

Seeing then, that the machinery of his talk remained intact in all its parts to his last days, it is plain that his last days were not passed in grinding misery; for no man in such circumstances has the freedom of mind necessary to talk well, and often with humour and wit, on a great variety of subjects. And, in fact, the legend of Wilde's last years ebbing out in squalor and destitution and abandonment should be discarded.

I read not long ago an association of the lives of Verlaine and Poe and Wilde. It never occurred to me, and it could not occur to anyone who knew them both, to compare Wilde with Verlaine. Verlaine, for the greatest part of his life, belonged to the outcast class. It was not poverty, forced on him by events over which he had no control, that brought him down; it was an interior degradation of the forces of his soul, the result, no doubt, of some natal curse. Even in his years of comparative respectability, before his imprisonment, he shewed whither he was tending. Verlaine could never have had the worldly success of Wilde because he was entirely helpless before the world and knew no more how to mould it to his will than a three years' child. His wants in his later days, as his miserable letters reveal them, were the wants of men harboured in night-refuges and workhouses—demands for a pair of shoes or a screw of tobacco or the price of a bottle. Perhaps, notwithstanding his fits of violence and drunkenness, Verlaine was a saint. He had many of the characteristics found in the lives of certain saints given as models for edification—humility, resignation, an indifference to worldly goods, a childlike, unquestioning religious faith. He was the greatest religious poet of modern times. He had very little intelligence. When he was not moved by his genius to write his poems, he was intellectually zero. Such prose as he has left signifies nothing. It is not even well put together. Compared with that of another great French poet of his time, Mallarmé, it is as a music-hall ditty to a nocturne of Chopin's.

Now to take Poe. The conditions of his life and the circumstances in which it was passed were so different from Wilde's that it is impossible to establish any relations between their physical or mental states. What seems to be a justified conclusion, after all the talk about his spasms of drink, his quarrelsome temper, his sexual inhibitions,[4] is that the real trouble with Poe, as with Villiers de l'Isle-Adam, was simply that editors and publishers did not consider him worth their money. They refused to pay him enough for his writings to enable him to live decently.

There came a time, as I have shewn, when Wilde could not write, but while he could write, especially for the stage, he could command a good deal of money, and without giving himself much trouble. He advised me to write plays. I said it seemed to me very difficult. He answered that he found nothing so easy. He had a full, even a gross sense of what the public liked and could assimilate. He had the face of a man born to popular success, even as Poe had the face of one born to misfortune; and he would have been a perfectly enormous success but for the accident that derailed him. For it was an accident; there was nothing in his character which made against success. He happened to live in a country which had a law against a certain form of vice which other countries tolerate. He came in conflict with that law and he was wrecked. He had to bear the stigma of the prison, with circumstances of cruelty and ignominy peculiar to his case alone. But all that was exterior to him, as a beam laid across the rails is exterior to the express train which it wrecks. That the beam is there says nothing against the perfect adjustment of the express train, its power to make seventy miles an hour. And it is just that which the spectator has in mind when he regards the shattered train turned over in a ditch.

---

[4] For a full-dress discussion of Poe from the point of view of the psychoanalyst, see the book of the Princess Marie Bonaparte (Princess George of Greece), published in Paris in 1934.

Vincent O'Sullivan

* * *

Of course, it may be said that this very faculty which Wilde displayed almost from the time when he was an undergraduate of gauging the public taste, of according himself with it, of interesting the public in the parade of his life, and of giving it what it wanted while seeming to despise it, indicated a certain vulgarity and was a proof that as an artist he was far from being in the first rank. Lionel Johnson, who did not like Wilde, used to speak in that way about him. Certainly, Wilde cannot be held to be a writer of the first order; but that he knew how to get the attention of the public, and got it early, proves nothing for or against him. *Pickwick* was popular from the day it was published; it is, nevertheless, a really great epic. Baudelaire's poems were prosecuted by the government of Napoleon III, which had all and rather more of the prudishness generally ascribed to Victorian England. For fifty years they lay in a sort of limbo, read by very few, and were considered by their admirers altogether too good for the public. Shortly after the war, the rights of the publisher lapsed; cheap editions appeared and were bought up like butter; and to-day Baudelaire's verses are printed on sentimental postcards like Longfellow's or Kipling's.

* * *

A thing to note is that Wilde, who was a Romantic, took the Romantic point of view. The Romantic point of view was that the poet is vowed to disaster; or, if the wine of success comes to him in a brimming goblet, it turns to ashes as he drinks. As already said, like Dostoevsky he came to regard in a mystic sense all that had happened to him. In his last years, when no doubt he felt that all was over, the two figures he was readiest to talk about, whom it seemed he could not help talking about, were Napoleon and Jesus Christ.

For Napoleon he thought St. Helena was necessary as the crown of his life. To end in a palace would have been too commonplace. On a rock, chained, must die the hero, after all that was petty and mean and cowardly has stung him and preyed upon his vitals. And the young god who had tried to teach beauty and peace and love to men, after the fields had been blessed by the passing of his feet, must have them nailed to the bitter wood, and be lifted up on the slave's cross for the derision of the city, and go down among the dead. For the just man is slain.

Yes, there is something vulgar in all success. It is in the vulgarest epochs, such as that we are now living in, it is in the coarsest manifestations of civilization, that blatant success is most esteemed.

* * *

All that is doubtless true. But Wilde was one of the men of success; he was born for it and it came to him, not tardily after long struggles, but at once. I have often thought that he would have had even more success, and his faculties fuller play, in this post-war period, driving up against the gale towards another war. He was by no means a shrinking flower, and the shrinking flower gets the worst of it to-day.

But seeing what he was, and what came upon him, it is easy enough to understand the part he drew from the life and death of Jesus and Napoleon. (The apposition of these two names is his, not mine.) The passion in the garden was an assault of the powers of evil; for if Christ had put away the chalice from his lips, *as he might have done*, the cross would never have been lifted up. Napoleon might have done better than give himself to the English; but his fate sent him on board their warship that his destiny might be fulfilled, and the lonely figure, beaten and discrowned, standing on the rock in the midst of the ocean, might live for ever in the hearts of men.

* * *

It was, no doubt, some such reasoning going on in his subconscious being which caused that reluctance, so puzzling to the few who were faithful to him, to employ the means of escape before he was imprisoned. It was even said that when the scandal began the police would have given him ample latitude to get out of England if he had chosen to take it. *Dabo tibi coronam vitae*: that was the voice he heard in the long days of agony between his trials; and the crown of life for him was the crown of thorns.

Consider what he would mean to the world without his passion. He might just possibly have broken new ground, done something better than anything he had yet done. But I think that extremely unlikely. He had never had any hindrances, and he had expressed himself as a prosperous man to the full. He would, then, have gone on writing popular and amusing and dramatic plays as long as his physical power remained intact. He would have left a memory of the same value as Sheridan's, no more and no less—that of another brilliant Irishman who had amused and perhaps served the English. He would have had the same kind of renown outside the English-speaking countries as Sheridan—that is to say, hardly any at all.

By his passion he was brought to say what *the unprosperous man* had it in him to say. It so happened that this utterance was not large or prolonged, for if his passion kindled a flame, it also killed him. Still, by many he is valued, not for his wit, but for *De Profundis* and the *Ballad*, fruits of his passion. He developed into that great tragic figure known in every part of the earth, whose cruel fate will be sorrowed by thousands for long years to come.

V

Like other gods and heroes, legends have formed about his name. It were better to let them be. His legend is often the definite explanation of a man. But the legend that Wilde's last years were spent in a squalor and degradation such as Verlaine's, and that his friends had let him fall into the gutter, should be annihilated, for it adds nothing to his figure and is quite untrue, even as a symbol.

* * *

That he was sometimes badly in need of money is certain. He had always been used to spending money freely. In his days of success, whenever he happened to be out of money he knew he could get a good sum without much trouble; and his wife had some fortune. It is extremely hard for men or women who have lived in such conditions to bring themselves down to living on a few hundred pounds a year. They don't know how to organize their lives on that basis; they don't know where to begin.

If Wilde had always been used to living on narrow means he could have managed very well in the years that followed his imprisonment. He had more money at his disposal than many of the young French writers and painters of that time. But they had simple tastes; they had never known anything better than to eat their meals in a little corner drink-shop, served by a sweating scullery-wench, and to live in small rooms opening on a courtyard. That suited their purse and did not outrage their tastes. But that sort of thing, comprehensibly enough, filled Wilde with disgust. He was past the age when such experiences can be taken with a light heart. And he had, furthermore, an utter loathing, an incredible horror of cheap restaurants and cheap lodgings. This was something more than physical repulsion; it was the revolt of his aesthetic sense. One day, Leonard Smithers, publisher, in an unwonted fit of economy proposed to take us to lunch at a restaurant which was not certainly very brilliant, but which was not a shabby place either. Wilde took a very high tone with him.

"My dear Smithers," he said, "don't be ridiculous. As an English tourist in Paris you simply can't go to such places. I forbid you."

Charles Conder, the painter, shared these lofty views. He complained to me of a certain English couple who had invited him to dinner in Paris: "I don't care to go with them," he said. "They bore me. They hunt out the cheap restaurants, and boast of it when they find one."

* * *

The Paris hotel in which Wilde lived and finally died was certainly not luxurious, but neither was it miserable or squalid. It was a good enough little place for those who are indifferent to surroundings or have schooled themselves to be contented with little. After the war, and before the Depression and Roosevelt-dollars, whole droves of Americans, who thought they were "bohemian" and seeing life, invaded the old Latin Quarter and its little hotels, although they could perfectly well afford to pay the prices of the big hotels. Those people I cannot understand. I cannot understand why people who have the means to pay for a room and bath and good service, should go to places where there is but one general bath-tub and no service worth mentioning. But one in Wilde's position has not any choice, and he might have fallen worse. Once he sent me a message to say that he would go mad if he were obliged to remain in his hotel that evening. "I can't spend the afternoon and evening in this hotel; it is so *triste* and yellow."

But he would have been seldom content to sit quietly through the evening in the best hotel in France. One day, during the Exposition year, he asked me how I had spent the previous evening. I answered that I had remained in my room in my hotel.

He looked at me curiously: "Were you alone?"

"Yes."

"Were you ill?"

"Oh, no."

He was seriously distressed, even annoyed.

"Think of it! In Paris, at your age, to waste an evening in a room in an hotel! What do you expect to do with your life?"

* * *

Meanwhile, he was always well dressed when I saw him, well shaved, and he was invariably punctual. That was one of his forms of good manners. He did not bear the expression of all he had suffered; there was nothing humiliated or downcast in his air. His immense vitality, and, no doubt, an innate sense of his superiority and real value, supported him. He was, in fact, imposing—far more imposing and self-assured in his carriage than many of the poor creatures who thought they would be lowering themselves if they were seen in his company. At times indeed his face would be swept with poignant anguish and regret when he had touched on some subject which brought back upon his heart his past joys and powers, or his hours of agony and humiliation, or the apprehension of his future, which he saw as a mountain-pass under darkling shadows falling ever thicker—becoming in fact, save by miracle, impracticable for him. At such moments he would pass his large hand with a trembling gesture over his face and stretch out his arm as though to ward off the phantom of his destiny. Doubtless with one of his very intimate friends, which I never was, that anguish often took shape in words. But this could not have been often.

What he was readier to put forward were the exterior tribulations of his life. It is absolutely certain that the only possible life for him in Paris depended upon his having enough money to keep him above the shifts and degradations of poverty. With his reputation, *as it appeared then*, to have the atmosphere of poverty brought him an added contempt, and left him no protection from the insults of the low-minded, who would have hesitated before a man protected by money, but saw no reason to treat decently a man who sometimes had to ask credit for his dinner, and even for a drink.

One day, when he had particularly abounded in this sense, I told him that Richard Wagner, who had a like horror of the mediocre in domestic affairs, would hire a large house, fill it with expensive things, and then trust to Liszt to find the money, or to the gifts of large-hearted and admiring ladies, and generous financiers such as Otto Wesendonck. He said their money was well spent; but he did not seem to have any hope of a like outcome for himself. The conditions were not the same, and Robert Ross as comptroller of finances was not so tolerant and easy-going as Liszt.

I never understood how his financial affairs were established. As far as I know, he was paid a monthly pittance supplied altogether, or in the largest part, by Miss Schuster, one of the rich banking family. I do not know what this amount was, but it had to be eked out by contributions from others. Ross, no doubt, did what he thought best, but his system may be estimated by what he once said to me: "I tell everybody not to give Oscar money. If you give him anything, give him clothes." Ross persuaded people that it was better that all sums destined for Oscar should pass through his hands. Wilde would say with a sigh: "Robbie is a dear, but he does not understand." He preferred that any money he received outside the Ross administration should not be mentioned to Ross. The Ross system was probably wrong. It left Wilde with long stretches of sheer destitution and panic, and horrible uncertainty about his future. There were certainly days in Paris when Wilde had nothing to eat, and for drink had to depend on acquaintances picked up in a little bar, "Calisaya," or some such place. It is a curious mark of his character that although he would borrow a few francs from his landlord or his washerwoman, he never addressed himself to those Frenchmen, friends of his prosperous days, who had made no sign of sympathy in his misfortune.

I have often wondered that more women did not aid Wilde, for I have always found, and find to-day, his warmest admirers among women. He, in his turn, admired women. I never heard him say anything disparaging about any woman, even when some of them required such treatment. He had an elaborate courteousness in dealing with them, out of fashion among young men at the time I knew him, and quite dead to-day.

Is it not in one of his plays that he says that a man should speak to every woman as though he were in love with her? Perhaps nearer to his thought was what he once said to me:

"The real Don Juan is not the vulgar person who goes about making love to all the women he meets, and what novelists call 'seducing' them. The real Don Juan is the man who says to women: 'Go away! I don't want you. You interfere with my life. I can do without you.' Swift was the real Don Juan. Two women died for him."

"One lived for him, which was perhaps worse."

"Yes. At any rate, she died to the world for him."

* * *

One woman, at least, did help Oscar Wilde out of sheer admiration for his gifts, and no doubt out of pity for his sad lot. This was the Miss Schuster I have mentioned, and her name should be remembered with the Metternichs, Kalergis, Pourtalès, Ritters, Wesendoncks, and other figures of women who adorn the Wagner epic. I think more men would have come to Wilde's relief if they had not dreaded that their names would leak out and their act be interpreted as sympathy, or, at best, condoning with his vice. Stuart Merrill, the French-American poet, who had been a friend of Wilde's in the days of his renown, but avoided seeing him after his imprisonment, must have been influenced by such reasons;

and there were many others. What seems to me iniquitous is that most of these people knew perfectly well Wilde's reputation at the time they were eager to be seen in his company. When he came to public misfortune they disowned him.

Stuart Merrill took the position that if he had known Wilde's sexual perversion at the time he kept company with him, he would have ceased all intercourse then and there. It is hard to believe that he did not know what his friend Gide so well knew. And if Oscar himself made little concealment in London, he made none at all in Paris.

To-day it is hard to realize the storm of contumely which fell on Wilde, out of all proportion, as it seems now, to the offence, and even to the real importance of the man. If he had attempted to steal the Crown Jewels, like Colonel Blood, or to blow up Queen Victoria and her Parliament assembled, like another Guido Fawkes, he could not have been more, or more publicly, vituperated. As to defending him, save in a very safe collection of friends, how few dared that! Even Sir Edward Clarke, the famous barrister who assumed the thankless and heavy task of defending Wilde, was blamed and reviled in some quarters.

This spirit did not prevail only in England. The most ignorant and brutal attacks on Wilde came from America. The French, among whom he chose to live out his final years, dealt with him according to their temperament, just as the English did. They allowed him to live as he liked, but they tolerated his presence rather than welcomed it. They did absolutely nothing to make his burden easier. His presence was often resented in public places. Some places he was insolently forbidden to enter. I heard that Catulle Mendès, finding Wilde at some huge banquet of a hundred and more, made a great fuss, squalled that he was insulted, and left the room. Now and then a poisonous little paragraph about Wilde would appear in the French papers.

Many of those in France, as in England, who had sought most eagerly his company in the days of his glory, now denied him.

They would look the other way if they saw him coming. Some of them, long after his death, having recovered from their panic, developed into great admirers of Wilde. Robert Ross, speaking to me one day of such men, who in their time had denounced not only Wilde, but Aubrey Beardsley and some others, and had since become admirers, collectors, and God knows what, said of them, quoting Meredith's line: "They eat their pot of honey on a grave."

* * *

When one considers that Wilde never held any position in what is called the public service, that for the public at large all that was known of his life's achievement were a few plays, the radiation which his wreckage had is inexplicable. In my first chapter I have spoken of magic; I have even heard it ascribed to the devil. His mother, to whom he seemed devoted, disowned him from the first hour of the scandal and said he was possessed by the Spirit of Evil.

What degree of turpitude lay in Wilde's fault has been much discussed and variously estimated. Here it is well to bear in mind the saying of Quintilian: "Only with modesty and circumspection should such men be judged." But it is not honourable to human nature that if Wilde had been guilty of a far greater crime, if he had ruined a number of people who had trusted him with all their means of living, and so had become responsible for the sins, insanities, suicides, and all the other manifold afflictions which such frauds invariably bring in their train, even to generations, he would have been far less insulted and reviled and humiliated; he would have found defenders and friends; nor, after he came forth from prison, would he have been shunned as a leper.

His story, *Hans and His Wheelbarrow*, under its lightness and grace, is a satire which, contrary to his wont, is scathing; and it might have been addressed by anticipation to some of his whilom friends.

One day he spoke to me this dreadful sentence: "It is what we fear that happens to us."

Disraeli thought otherwise. According to him, what men fear does not often happen, but the fear itself corrodes and demoralizes. In Wilde's life there was no sign, so far as I know, that he had the least apprehension of his ultimate disaster. But there is a story of his, written while he was still a young man, called *Lord Arthur Savile's Crime*. At an evening party a soothsayer, called in to entertain the guests, predicts to Lord Arthur Savile that he will one day commit a crime. This prediction weighs on the young man; the thought of it poisons his life of pleasure. One night he encounters the soothsayer in the street, entices him on to one of the London bridges, and flings him into the Thames to drown. So is the prophecy fulfilled and Lord Arthur delivered from his obsession.

It is characteristic of Wilde that he does not treat this terrible imagination tragically, as Poe or Barbey d'Aurevilly would have treated it. His story is written in a burlesque tone, and thus weakened. But I have often thought that it might have some basis in fact—I mean, that he may have passed his life up to the hour of his arrest under the weight of some prediction heard in early youth. He believed in omens. He told me that as a child he heard the Banshee, and woke up crying: "Why are they beating that dog? Tell them to stop beating the dog."

The next day one of the family died.

His mother died while he was in prison. He told me quite seriously that on the night of her death she appeared to him in his cell. She was dressed for out-of-doors, and he asked her to take off her hat and cloak and sit down. But she shook her head sadly and vanished. When they came to tell him of her death he said quietly: "I knew it already."

At Naples he pointed out to me in the street an old woman. "Unless that old woman asks you for money do not offer it to her. But if she asks you, be sure not to refuse." Some days later we were sitting in a restaurant when the witch came by. She paused a moment, looked at us both steadfastly, and then went her way. Wilde was very much disturbed. "Did you see that? She has looked in at the window. Some great misfortune is going to happen to us."

And who knows, in those old lands where the necromancers of Virgil have left their secrets?

So it is not impossible that a dismal prediction heard in youth gave him vague disquiet, and that he wrote his story to get it out of his mind—to reduce it, if he could, to nonsense.

* * *

He died in the Catholic Church, being baptized *in articulo mortis*. But if he died in the Church, he did not live in it. From my knowledge of Wilde I have never been able to reconstruct the steps which brought him to Catholicism. No doubt, outside influence counted for something. Robert Ross, who was beside him when he died, was a Catholic convert, with the proselytizing zeal seen more often in converts than in born Catholics. But from his early days Wilde had shown the same kind of aesthetic sympathy with Catholicism, with its pageantry and historical side, which is found in Pater. There is a sonnet of his, written in Italy when he was a very young man, in which he says that when he recalled that "in Rome in chains the second Peter lay, he wept to see the land so very fair." On the other hand, he had that rather morbid horror of the unloveliness of certain aspects of Protestantism which Matthew Arnold has expressed in his famous comparison of Eugénie de Guérin with an Evangelical lady of Brighton. He told me that Arthur Balfour once asked him what was his religion. "Well, you know," replied Wilde, "I don't think I have any. I am an Irish Protestant."

In the "Eighteen-Nineties," as anybody can see who reads the characteristic literature of the young writers of that time,

Catholicism was in favour and Protestantism decidedly was not. Some, Beardsley, Lionel Johnson, Ernest Dowson, Mrs. Craigie ("John Oliver Hobbes"), responding to one impulse or another, were "received," as the phrase is, into the Catholic Church. Some Jews, even, were caught up by the stream. Newman counted for something in these conversions; Pater, and the revolt against Victorianism, for a good deal. Wilde, I am sure, counted for nothing.

How could he? His philosophy is pagan. The practical side of Catholicism, with its obligation to a certain order of life and to certain devotions, would have bored him. Before the Catholic devotion and its images—the stabbed, bleeding, and excruciated figure, the heart dripping blood, the woman's heart with a knife in it—he would have felt as strange and disconcerted as one of the young woodland gods who haunted the sacred groves in Thessaly. He knew little about theology, and the theological mind he abhorred. All he had retained out of Newman was the passage about the snapdragon under the windows of Trinity. He never with me, and, I should think, not with anybody, discussed Christianity as a devotional exercise or as a means of saving one's soul alive. All that lay outside the circle of his interests. When he spoke of Christianity as an historical revelation he became "sketchy," and even sometimes took a burlesque attitude.

One day he undertook to explain the persecution of the early Christians in Rome.

"You know, Nero was obliged to do something. They were making him ridiculous. What he thought was: 'Here everything was going on very well, when one day two incredible creatures arrived from somewhere in the provinces. They are called Peter and Paul, or some unheard-of names like that. Since they are here, life in Rome has become impossible. They collect crowds and block the traffic with their miracles. It is really intolerable. I, the Emperor, have no peace. When I get up in the morning and look out of the window, the first thing I see is a miracle going on in the back garden.'"

* * *

In Amiel, in Pater, even in Matthew Arnold, whatever their ultimate attitude towards Christianity, is obvious the anxiety, which in Pater goes even to anguish, of those who seek for a certainty, an abiding place for their soul, *Inquietum est cor nostrum, donec requiescat in te*, said one in the same case, St. Augustine. The coarser nature of Wilde protected him from such tribulations. Coarser nature, but also happier nature. From that desolate and crushing anxiety arising from causes so remote that they can hardly be expressed, that feeling of the barrenness of all effort and of the miserable human fate, which has so cruelly assailed certain artists, Wilde seemed entirely free.

When Pater came to London to give a lecture, the audience saw a short solid man with a white heavy Dutch face, square chin, thick moustache and little cautious eyes, not placid, for lights of disquiet and even of temper would pass in their guarded depths. From such a presence, to the surprise of some, though indeed the rotund figure did suggest pensiveness rather than brawl, the voice fell softly. At the end, said Pater: "I was rather afraid that people had not heard me." "We overheard you," answered the ready Oscar, perhaps a little disdainfully.

For *he* had always his faculties at command and at immediate command—all the social faculties—and they seemed to him too easy to lack. There can be no doubt that this jocund imperviousness, this unfamiliarity with the land of twilight and shadows, counted for much in his worldly success; and what is more, was of aid to him when his luck broke. Other men from such an experience would have emerged stupefied and crushed. Wilde was not crushed at all. He had to a very unusual degree the gift of putting away from him by a turn of imagination what his physical organization revolted against.

"There is here at Naples," he said one evening, "a garden where those who have determined to kill themselves go. A short time ago, after Bosie had gone away, I was so cast down by the boredom of leaving the villa at Posilipo, and by the annoyance that some absurd friends in England were giving me, that I felt I could bear no more. Really, I came to wish that I was back in my prisoner's cell picking oakum. I thought of suicide."

"You?"

"Does that surprise you?"

"Yes—that is, I think that suicide is impossible for you now. It should have come before—much before—if at all."

"I was never really tempted to kill myself. I never thought seriously of that as a way out. What I felt was that I must drain the chalice of my passion to the dregs. But one night when there were no stars I went down to that garden. As I sat there absolutely alone in the darkness, I heard a rustling noise, and sighing; and misty cloud-like things came round me. And I realized that they were the little souls of those who had killed themselves in that place, condemned to linger there ever after. They had killed themselves in vain. And when I thought that such would be the fate of my soul too, the temptation to kill myself left me and has not come back."

It will be observed that it was pressure of circumstances which forced him to think of suicide. It was not *taedium vitae* as with Beddoes, or a horror of his own soul as with van Gogh, or seeing his madness face to face as with Gérard de Nerval. It was nothing interior. Did he even think of it seriously?

"The 'Lord Illingworths' do not commit suicide," I said. "How could you imagine spending all your life after life in Naples?"

He laughed: "No, the cooking is really too bad."

* * *

He could ignore what he did not like, what hurt him, or what simply did not suit him. All of us, I suppose, try to do this, and many pretend to be able to do it. Wilde really could do it. One reason was that he had no self-consequence to be mortified, for self-consequence and ordinary conceit had long ago become blended in an unshakable estimation of his own value, which was something quite different from conceit. A god wandering among men could not be accused of vanity because he felt his godhead put him above the run of men. That was how Wilde felt; and no prison, no humiliation, could alter his conception of himself. It was long after his imprisonment that he spoke to me with some disgust of a scene he had witnessed at a public dinner in Paris. A well-known poet had made a row because he had not been placed at the high-table. "Could anything be more petty—a greater revelation of insignificance? Now for me, the highest place is where I am myself."

One afternoon in Dieppe, Wilde, with Conder, Ross, Smithers, myself, and one or two others were seated in a modest restaurant. A Frenchman with his wife and a child of four or five were at a near table, and this Frenchman, feeling somehow that his dignity as a father of a family was outraged by the presence of Wilde, called the head-waiter and objected. The head-waiter came and whispered to Wilde, who turned to me and said: "It seems *the child* objects to smoking." With that he got up and walked out, and the rest of us followed him. Wilde did not seem disturbed by this affront. At that time I gave so little attention to contingencies that I should indeed have been unaware of what had happened if Conder had not told me afterwards, for Wilde himself had uttered no word of complaint at the scurvy treatment.

It has often occurred to me since that he could get outside of himself and consider as a spectator the spectacle of his life. He told me that at an evening party in London, when he was at the height of his fame, Hubert Crackanthorpe, a young man who had just published a little book of stories, came up to him and asked:

"What do you think of my work, Mr. Wilde?" "Your play, dear boy, your play," replied Wilde. He laughed heartily as he told this, and then went on as though speaking of another: "The great dandy who had just come in to get rid of a few minutes, and was going on to another party, saying indifferently as he was putting on his coat: 'Your play, dear boy, your play.'"

He had Horace Walpole's weakness: he strongly objected to being considered a professional author. Like Walpole, he preferred to be thought a man of fashion who wrote when time hung heavy on his hands and he had nothing better to do. In Horace Walpole there was much more plausibility for such an attitude than in Wilde; though it is true that till he hit the public with his plays Wilde made little or no money by his writings, if we except *Dorian Gray*, which, I believe, sold well, and may have earned money for the author as well as for the publisher. But it is just as likely that he sold the copyright for a small sum, for at the time he published *Dorian Gray* he was not considered a money-making author. He hated to talk of money in connection with his books. It must have been some odd remainder of Victorian class-prejudice which made him resent being called an author. He always spoke of himself as an artist. Where the advantage lies it is hard to see.

One day he said to me: "I was thinking in bed this morning that the great superiority of France over England is that in France every bourgeois wants to be an artist, whereas in England every artist wants to be a bourgeois." This was a part of the Romanticism of which he had his full share. For in France, give most artists a little success, that is to say some money, and they take to themselves wives and enter the bourgeois class with remarkable alacrity. "Look at Tennyson," Wilde added. "Could there be an existence more deplorable for a poet than such an existence as Tennyson's?" Yet he admired Tennyson, who, he said, chose words as he would jewels out of a casket.

Ernest Dowson told something about Wilde which surprised me rather. He said he went to see Wilde one evening at the

Berkeley Hotel in Piccadilly. It was quite early in the evening, but he found Wilde in bed propped up with pillows and engaged in pasting newspaper clippings about himself into a large scrapbook. What surprised me in this story was that Wilde ever cared enough about what other people said of him to think their opinions worth preserving. Perhaps he only contemned the opinion of the world when that opinion was disagreeable to him. I said to him once: "I suppose one of the reasons which led you to write plays was that you wanted the immediate applause?" He paused a moment, and then replied deliberately: "Yes, the immediate applause. What a charming phrase of yours." He rolled it on his tongue. "The immediate applause."

Marcel Schwob, the well-known French writer, gave me an instance of Wilde regarding himself as a spectacle. One morning he went to see Wilde in Paris. Wilde had just finished dressing and was going out to lunch. He looked about for his cane. "My gold-headed cane has disappeared. Last night I was with the most terrible creatures, bandits, murderers, thieves—such company as Villon kept. They stole my gold-headed cane. There was a youth with beautiful sad eyes who had slain his mistress that morning because she was unfaithful. I feel sure it was he who stole my gold-headed cane." He spoke with relish and satisfaction.

"My gold-headed cane is now between the hands that slew the frail girl who had the grace of a spent rose-bush in the rain."

Schwob meanwhile had been looking about the room, and spied the cane in a corner. "But, Mr. Wilde, *there* is your gold-headed cane."

"Ah, yes!" said Wilde, horribly disappointed; "so it is! There is my gold-headed cane. How clever of you to find it."

* * *

He gave me as an explanation of his attraction to a certain rather commonplace English journalist, that he had the face of Octavius on the coins. Nobody else could see the resemblance. One day, about a year before his trial, I met him in the Café Royal in London. He seemed rather upset. "There is a dreadful youth waiting for me in Regent Street. He is pacing up and down before the door like a wonderful black panther. I think he must be there yet. Do go and see. If he is, I shall go out by the side door." Accordingly, I went out on Regent Street and glanced around me. I did see a young fellow hanging about who looked like a rather disquieting specimen of London vegetation, but who had nothing at all in him to suggest, to me at least, the grace and ease of a beautiful black panther.

Wilde carried his transmutation of values to names. If he did not like a name he altered it or mispronounced it. He sent Lionel Johnson his *Dorian Gray* with this curious inscription: "To Lionel, with the writer's compliments." That was his way of showing that he liked Lionel but not Johnson. Arthur Symons' name, for some reason I could never grasp, he persistently mispronounced, calling him Simons, with the *i* long. "But he calls himself Simmons," I said.

"How can you be so childish! It is perfectly clear that Simons doesn't know how to pronounce his own name."

He did not like the writings of Arthur Symons, but as Symons wrote the best article that appeared on the publication of *The Ballad*, he felt obliged to rectify his attitude towards the poet of *London Nights*. He advanced the theory that there was a syndicate which produced a mass of printed matter under the corporate name of Arthur Symons. "I have written to my solicitor to inquire about shares in Symons Ltd." He added: "Naturally in mass productions of that kind you can never be certain of the quality. But I think one might risk some shares in Symons."

An actress who played in one of his plays was reputed to have a physiological inversion like to his own, and he said of her amusingly enough: "Dear——, she is one of Nature's gentlemen."

Max Beerbohm he invariably called Max, but then everybody else did at that time. Of him Wilde said to me, and perhaps to others: "The gods bestowed on Max the gift of perpetual old age."

* * *

It is impossible to avoid speaking of his snobbery, which was very marked. He was often bantered about it during his lifetime. Snobbery is not so simple or so easy to analyse as Thackeray fancied. There are many varieties of it, and it proceeds from many causes. The French are not often snobs in the English sense of the word; the Americans very often are. Brookfield (I think it was) used to say that Oscar was a snob because he came from a family of Irish Unionists, the most snobbish people on earth. Wilde's snobbery would thus be of the same nature as that of the professor in Trinity College, Dublin, who wrote of Richard Steele that he was never ashamed of his country, and so revealed what is called an inferiority complex.

The objection to those who explain Wilde in this way is that Wilde never considered the Irish inferior to the English. That such an opinion had course in his earlier time in England, and among the English-Americans, he ascribed as I once heard him say, to "the insolence with which the English have always treated us," and also to the fact that the Irish among the English-language races was the Catholic race, the race which had not accepted the Reformation of the sixteenth century.

However that may be, he himself, I thought, was very Irish in aspect and methods—much more indeed than he suspected. I often used to think that the great Irishmen of the eighteenth century who exercised such a fascination on the English, Burke, Congreve, Steele, Sheridan, must have been in many ways like him, and that he was of their line. But he would also sometimes remind me of that extraordinary "Father Prout," who was also great and magical. That was on the good side. On the other, he was a disagreeable reminder, often enough, of Thomas Moore.

Ireland is not explicitly in his writings any more than it is in Goldsmith's, but as with Goldsmith, I think it is implicitly there, though perhaps not to the same extent, for Goldsmith was Anglo-Irish, whereas Wilde on his father's side descended from a Dutch follower of William of Orange. He did not seem particularly proud of this; at least, he liked to say that he took after his mother's family, which, it seems, was pure Irish, more than his father's. The too grandiloquent pseudonym he adopted when he was released from prison, Sebastian Melmoth, he took in part from a forgotten novel, *Melmoth, the Wanderer*, written by an Irish kinsman of his mother's, a contemporary of Byron, named Maturin. He told me that to a very eminent Englishman who said to him that in the nineteenth century the Mac's had done everything and the O's nothing, he answered: "You forget. There are O'Connell and O. Wilde."

He admired O'Connell, and praised Balzac for placing him among the three principal figures of the first half of the nineteenth century. Parnell also he admired.

He has been blamed by some for not putting Irish things into his writing, for not making them definitely Irish. Because he did not do that I have seen him treated as a writer of no importance, "a second-rate literary man," with other compliments on the same scale of intelligence. There have been writers in all countries whose writings bear no trace of geographical or ethnical accidents. Except for his plays, which reflect a superficial—very superficial English life, Wilde wrote in a vacuum. His works have value not as pictures of life in a given place, but as pictures of ideas. The ideas are not always first-rate; but what of that? It is not the idea in itself which counts, but the power which lies within it to excite and inspire. It was as alien to his genius as to the genius of Watteau to give realistic pictures of life in Ireland or anywhere. From the kind of criticism which pronounces flatly that a writer is worthless, "a second-rate literary man," because he did not do what the critic would like him to have done, all reasonable people must shrink.

To speak generally of Wilde's snobbishness: It was not of the same order as the degrading and miserable details of social intercourse, where all human dignity goes by the board, on which Thackeray misspent so much trouble. In most cases snobbery proceeds from the uncertain sense which some men and women have of their own value, and this leads them to seek the countenance of those whose value is accepted and certain, this value being generally quite conventional and exterior, a matter of titles or riches. Now, Wilde, as we have seen, had an immense realization of his own value. His snobbery, then, could not have arisen from any need to prop up his sense of his own importance. It was rather a part of his general character, going with his love of gorgeous habitations and a life from which all distressing and sordid episodes were excluded.

One day I took it on myself to tell him that I thought there were too many people of title in his plays.

"You would permit at least a Colonial Knight?" he asked, rather nettled. Then he added: "And do you think Shakespeare has too many people of title in his plays?"

"No. But it is only here and there that Shakespeare tries to represent the life of his time. By the nature of his subjects they could only work themselves out in the highest section of human society. He had as much need of kings and princesses and courtiers as the Greek dramatists of the gods, as Milton of God-the-Father, and Satan, and the angels. Ben Jonson, who did set himself to represent the life of Shakespeare's time, is very sparing of titles in his comedies. Now, your plays too are offered as pictures of the life of your time. Of course, I know that in England the titled class is large, and that it is, to a certain extent, blended with the general life of the country. But from your plays one would infer that there was nothing else but the aristocratic—or rather the titled class; its servants; and some parasites. That, after all, is one of the causes of the success of your plays. The aristocrats go to see them to learn how aristocrats are supposed to behave, and the rest of the public to learn how they do."

"Is that how you feel about my plays?" he said. He looked about as though something else had taken his attention, and ended the subject by saying: "I think you must allow me a Colonial Knight in my next play."

That was perhaps a rebuke to a very young man for venturing to criticize to his face a man of his eminence. But to resent such things was not much in his way. He never, that I saw, assumed the air of the great master who must not be contradicted. It is true that he seldom was. But really I have seen more touchiness and self-importance in some little novelists and poets than Wilde ever shewed. No doubt he had his sore points, but his literary side was not one of them.

In his morbid ponderings upon snobbery, Thackeray worried out, among other definitions of a snob, this: "A snob is a man who will accept your invitation to dinner, and keep the engagement unless in the meantime he is invited by somebody he thinks more important." Wilde was perhaps capable of throwing over a dinner in a suburban villa to dine with a duke; but if he had been so placed that he had to choose between dining with a duke and dining with Ruskin, I am sure he would have chosen Ruskin.

* * *

I never could make out just where Wilde considered himself to rank in the social hierarchy of England. Sometimes he would put forward a claim that the artist is in his right place in the highest society. That was also the conclusion of Liszt who, like Wilde, and much more than Wilde, was received in the highest society, and thought that the way in which such society accepted him left something to desire. But Liszt approached the subject from another point than Wilde, and had personal and intimate reasons to be touchy about his standing which Wilde had not at all. And indeed Wilde never complained about the manner of his reception by English high society. On the contrary, he shewed a rather naïve satisfaction.

At times he was wont to talk loftily about "my class," and to dismiss certain people as not being in his class. And he did not mean his intellectual class, but his social class. Some, whom I thought quite all right, very good families and all that, I was surprised to see Wilde cast out as not belonging to his class. I once mentioned to him that I had met a certain man, whom he did consider to be in his class, at dinner at the house of some people in London that I, in my innocence, considered of quite as good social standing as Wilde's friend. But he expressed great astonishment that his friend should have been found dining with such people, who were not at all of his class. "However could he think of going there?" he asked slightingly. He spoke as if it were a boarding-house at Margate.

But the most curious thing of all had relation to Beardsley. When Wilde came out of prison, Beardsley and he were in Dieppe at the same time; but Beardsley, although, of course, he knew Wilde very well, refused to see him. Beardsley was receiving a pension from a man who was an enemy of Wilde, and it was quite possible that if he had gone to see Wilde the pension would have been withdrawn. The amount of the pension I know not, but it could not have been adequate, even eked out with what Smithers paid for work done; for towards the end of his life, Beardsley, who was dragging out the last hours of a painful existence in second-rate Continental hotels and boarding-houses was sometimes obliged to ask for help elsewhere. Here, Wilde and not Beardsley is the subject; but it is impossible to write down such a fact without some expression of disgust and indignation that the greatest genius of the last years of the nineteenth century, young and dying, should have been in such a plight as to money. The fault was indirectly Wilde's, and directly Smithers'. After the Wilde scandal the London art publishers were shy of Beardsley, who was forced to rely on Smithers, and this man had neither the means nor the talent to put Beardsley properly before the public or to pay a fair price. He did his best, but his business was not organized as a publishing business, but more as a bookseller's—a bookseller who deals in rare editions.

However, what concerns us here is that Beardsley did not see Wilde at Dieppe or ever again in this world, though when he talked of him, it was in a very detached tone, certainly without any active dislike. But Wilde one day, much later, in Paris, broke out violently against Beardsley. "It was *lâche* of Aubrey," he said to me, and his voice and his hands trembled. "If it had been one of my own class I might perhaps have understood it. I don't know whether I respect most the people who see me or those who don't. But a boy like that, whom I made! No, it was too *lâche* of Aubrey."

Now, what is one to make out of that? What difference did he imagine there was between Beardsley's class and his own? For Beardsley was the artist, and, into the bargain, the genius. You could not be in his company five minutes without perceiving that you had before you a genius. Of Wilde's genius I am not so sure. The word *genius* is employed here in a strict sense, and not as understood by reviewers who plaster it on a hundred scribblers a year. Even if we leave aside the motives of artist and genius, it is hard to see any material difference between the social conditions Beardsley rose from and those which produced Wilde.

* * *

To whatever class Wilde considered he belonged, it may be said decidedly that he was by no means what is known as the "English-gentleman" type. He was perhaps something better; but that certainly he was not. He had good manners, was scarcely ever rude, admirably good-natured. But he had something about him of that excessive look seen in the pictures of men put on advertisements of health-foods, and cigarettes, and automobiles. From the English-gentleman point of view there was something a little wrong with him everywhere—in his appearance, and his clothes, and his manners. He never looked well-dressed; he looked "dressed up." In the upper reaches of English society it was not the men, who mostly did not like him, who made his success, but the women. He was too far from the familiar type of the men. He did not shoot or hunt or play cards; he had wit, and took the trouble to talk and be entertaining. He deluded himself if he really thought that the British aristocrats accepted him as one of themselves. One of them said to me quite sincerely and in disparagement that he had always thought there was something "foreign" about Wilde.

The curious thing is that he might quite easily have consolidated his position in English society through the one means by which the unwealthy have ever won a secure foothold therein. He had all the qualities that make a successful politician— brazen self-confidence, an impervious skin which defied scoffs and ridicule, an inexhaustible flow of language, and what is more, a far better head than most politicians are dowered with. But he took no interest in politics, the British Empire bored him except on its picturesque side, he had no stake in the country, and so he lost his chance of dominating the English aristocracy he so much admired. In fact, he rather lost his head about them, and so in a measure had less of their respect. If he had been useful to them, as Disraeli was, they might have accepted him—at least, to the same extent as they accepted Disraeli. But Wilde they looked on as a mere entertainer, who was sought after by the women because he was much more brilliant and amusing than anybody else they knew, and tolerated by the men because their womenkind imposed him. The way these men and women, almost without exception, dropped Wilde when his trial came, shews how little real hold he had on them.

Vincent O'Sullivan

* * *

A man as posterity sees him is hardly ever the real man. It is even hard to get an accurate picture of a man from more or less contemporary accounts. To my mind the best description in many respects—not in all—of Wilde is to be found in Lord Alfred Douglas's book, *Oscar Wilde and Myself*. The book is written in a spirit of animosity, for which there is considerable justification. But for all that the figure of Wilde emerges, perfectly recognizable. The book has nowhere received justice, because wherever the life of Wilde is discussed it is the fashion to give Douglas the wrong end of the stick, especially on the continent of Europe.

It is often said, for instance, that Douglas enticed Wilde to Naples with glittering promises and then heartlessly abandoned him. But Douglas depended on his mother for money. His mother came to Rome and threatened to cut off all supplies if he did not at once leave Naples and come to Rome. On the other side, Wilde's friends, and his wife's friends, were urging Wilde to separate from Douglas and threatening him with destitution if he continued to see Douglas. Is it any wonder that Douglas considered the situation impossible? He left for Rome with the intention, as I understood it, to get money from his mother and send it to Wilde. I don't know whether this money was sent or not; but it probably was. I came to Naples shortly after Douglas had gone away. Wilde spoke to me of certain grievances which he thought he had against Douglas. They were of a personal, not of a material, order, and seemed to me rather dramatized. He never blamed Douglas before me for leaving Naples; indeed, he seemed to think there was nothing else for him to do. That he had formed no implacable grudge against Douglas is certain, for I dined with them both a long time after in Paris.

It is usual with writers on Wilde to treat Douglas as insignificant, as one who only counts, and counts badly, by his connection with Wilde. The truth is that as a poet he is far superior to Wilde.

Personally I prefer his way of writing English prose to Wilde's. His prose is not gorgeous and decorated as Wilde's is; or sensual, sensational, and moving, as Wilde's can be too; but for polemic and narrative it is hard to beat.

VI

LET US LOOK A little at Wilde's declared enemies.

"Be careful to choose your enemies well," he said to me. "Friends don't much matter. But the choice of enemies is very important."

This saying, like most of his other sayings, contains what has made his philosophy a success throughout the world. Under the paradox is always a grain of truth, and sometimes a profound truth.

* * *

A man such as Wilde, become so famous and successful with what seemed so little effort, had naturally a host of enemies. With many of these, journalists like Clement Scott, for instance, he had as little personal relation as with the strumpets who danced in the streets outside the Old Bailey the day he was condemned. Clement Scott on the same occasion danced down a column of the *Daily Telegraph*. "Open the windows!" he cried. "Let in the fresh air!"

Some time before that, Wilde was grossly insulted in a club in London by another journalist. Not long after, this man fell on evil days and wrote to Wilde, of all people in the world, for his aid. Wilde sent him a cheque for a considerable sum. It was not Wilde himself who told me this—he would have been the last to do it—but someone, not friendly to Wilde, who knew the circumstances.

Among Wilde's enemies who had some figure must be reckoned W. E. Henley. Henley many people found intensely disagreeable. He was a brutal and embittered man. I suppose he had a good side which he shewed to his intimates, for I have known some who were devoted to him. It is said that he furnished Stevenson with some traits of the character "Pew" in *Treasure Island*, and that explains as well as anything the kind of man he was. Wilde and

Henley were bound to be at loggerheads. Two men more different were never made. Henley's brutal manners, his custom of snubbing and insulting people, were distasteful to Wilde, who was always considerate. Henley's imperialism, patrioteering, waving of the Union Jack, to Wilde said nothing at all. Henley, on his side, classed Wilde as an aesthete, by which he meant everything that is feeble and low.

When *The Ballad of Reading Gaol* appeared, Henley published a violent attack on the poem. I have heard, but I don't know how true it is, that he got out of this ugly business of kicking a man who was down by saying that if the poem had been badly received, he would have let it alone, but when he saw that it was a public success he determined to have his fling at it. As his article may not be available at present, it is worth while to mention at least one touch in it. Henley cited the lines:

> And blood and wine were on his hands
> When they found him with the dead.

"Ha, old truepenny!" exclaimed, in substance, Henley. "You cannot see clear now no more than you ever could. Your prison experience has taught you nothing. Aesthete you were and so remain. For what should *wine*, be it red or white, have to do on the hands of an English Tommy? 'Blood and *beer*' is more likely, but that is not pretty enough for you."

Wilde replied to Henley, but I have never seen what he wrote. He repeated to me with a certain relish a phrase in his reply: "To talk with him [Henley] is a physical as well as a mental recreation."

"My little reply is a very slight affair," he said. "I was at Compiègne. I wrote it as I was getting into a cab to go to the station."

As usual with him, he did not seem to have much resentment against Henley. "Henley owes me seven-and-six," he said some time later. "The other day I read a review of his praising a novel by somebody named Mary Cholmondeley. I bought the book, and before I had read very far, I came on this sentence: 'The birds were singing on every twig and on every little twiglet.' Now, you know, when an artist comes on a sentence like that in a book it is impossible for him to go on reading it. So I consider that Henley owes me seven-and-six."

But he often spoke respectfully of Henley, praising the strength of will which had enabled him to struggle against his disabling malady. He said once that Henley was the only man who had obliged him to put forth all his intellectual powers in conversation.

* * *

The Ballad, whatever immense fortune it has had, he himself did not put in a very high place among his writings. "I wrote to Robbie Ross the other day that I shall no longer try to out-Kipling Henley." To write it he had to violate all his theories of art. When he read it to me before it was published, he did so with great modesty and hesitation, which was quite extraordinary from a man of his intellectual position to a young man who had done nothing. "I feel quite sure you won't like it. I am not sure that I like it myself. But catastrophes in life bring about catastrophes in art."

He added several stanzas to the first draft, and, to my thinking, the additions were not always happy. After it was published he wrote me that he liked it better. "Print settles it, as Charles Lamb said." I suppose Lamb *has* said this somewhere, or something like it? It is the book of Wilde's best suited to the great reading public, which responds to the same kind of art as the great theatre and film public.

* * *

Another enemy of Wilde's was George Moore. There was no love lost between the two. Moore was one of the few people upon whom Wilde exercised his wit in a way that was sometimes cruel.

"Do you know George Moore?" I asked him one day when he had been rolling the British Zola's novels round the ring.

"Know him? I know him so well that I haven't spoken to him in ten years."

"He leads his readers to the latrines—and locks the door," was one of the amenities he bestowed on the author of *Esther Waters*—which Wilde persisted in calling "On the face of the Esther Waters."

As to the worth and interest of the writings of these two Irishmen, who were of an age, opinions will differ. As to which of them had the higher moral values in all that becomes a man, there can be no doubt whatever. Moore cared for art, and for no one or nothing else much, or for any length of time.

He has often been compared to Zola, called the British Zola—a term which he himself resented. But he had nothing of Zola's passionate interest in the broad questioning of life and the welfare of our general humanity. He could no more have written *Germinal* than he could have planned the excavation of a mine. Dreyfus would have lain forever on Devil's Island if he had waited till Moore risked fortune and liberty to save him as Zola did. Whom Moore took after and copied was not Zola, still less Flaubert, but the Goncourts, like him artists to the exclusion of all else. Like him the Goncourts began with painting, passed on to the Naturalistic novel and to writings on pictures and literature, and then turned to very personal Memoirs in which many of their friends and acquaintances were maltreated.

I was surprised to learn that he left so much money, for I had accounted for and excused many of his acts, and even the paper shirt-collars which at one time he wore, as the defences of a struggling author who was obliged to look twice at every penny he spent. But he turned out to be a rich man, and what would be considered a rich man in any commerce or profession. Was he mourned? Certainly those who live in any style at all above the waterline of stark poverty and its dismal degradation have usually a few who profit by them. But those apart, was Moore mourned as Wilde was mourned? Did he leave anybody who really cared two coppers for him? He died honoured and rich, eulogized by the newspapers. Wilde died in poverty and defeat, and the news of his death was huddled into a corner of the newspapers, as if a taint of disgrace attached to it too as well as to his life. Yet Wilde's moral value was as superior to that of George Moore as his imposing physical presence was superior to Moore's, which was mean. Wilde was often without money, but when he had it he was generous with it, as he was generous in all ways. Moore had petty meannesses, excusable sometimes in a man who has had a youth of poverty and hardship; for habits bred of privation and forcibly acquired in youth are not easily shaken off. But this was not Moore's case: he told me that there had been times when he had less money than at other times, but that never had he endured serious difficulty and anxiety from lack of money. Yet it was obviously a great effort for him to decide upon making the sacrifice of a shilling or two on a drink for an acquaintance. Far from the gracious and smiling hospitality of Wilde, who made everyone feel that he or she was just the person he desired, Moore was devoid of any notion of hospitality, to such an extent indeed that it led one to doubt if he had ever lived in surroundings where the most elementary social conventions prevailed. Twice, once in Paris and once in London, I came upon Moore in the street of an evening, and each time he said he was going to dine at a restaurant and invited me to dine with him. I thought I was his guest till he called for the bill and asked me to pay my share. Once in London Moore and myself were having a drink in the Café Royal after the theatre when an American publisher or book-agent came up to our table and spoke to Moore who asked him to sit down with us. After some talk Moore called the waiter and took out some money. He paid for our two drinks, and said to the American:

"You surely don't expect me to pay for what you have had? I did not ask you to have anything."

The man looked disconcerted and ashamed. "Why, certainly, Mr. Moore, I'll pay for my own drink, and I'll invite you to have another on me."

But Moore was already making for the door, and the rebuff did not hinder the man from saying to me that he thought Moore was the greatest writer alive.

You had only to listen to the talk of the two men and the moral and intellectual superiority of Wilde was manifest. Wilde treated of great subjects; he lifted up the souls of his listeners. Moore's talk at the best was the technical talk of the artist, but far more often and usually the talk of the professional author. It is astonishing, when one comes to think of it, how very few ideas of any value Moore ever expressed. I can't recall a single memorable thing he ever said. He liked also to talk about women, and particularly of the woman he happened at the moment to be reaching for. This he did with almost incredible coarseness. Wilde's talk was constantly chaste in my experience, and in the experience, I should think, of everybody.

One might surmise that in the mutual hate of these two Irishmen there was mingled some of the social prejudices peculiar to the Ireland of their time. In what is no doubt the only country left on earth where the adherents of two forms of the Christian religion are ready to slay one another, and often do, it is quite possible that class prejudice still exists. In an earlier time, the time of the youth of Wilde and Moore, it must have existed in an aggravated form, and Moore, the son of an Irish landowner, may have looked down on the son of the Dublin practitioner. Wilde, on his side, despised Moore as ignorant, not so much because of his ignorance as because he thought him bumptiously ignorant. "He is studying music," I said. "Yes; he conducts his education in the sight of the public." Somebody who was there put in: "After all, the public pay for it. They have a right to know how he is getting on."

Moore, taking up the study of music when he was past forty, the study of the origin of Christianity and of the mediaeval Church when he was past sixty, seems in this to have the better of Wilde, who stayed as to knowledge where he was when he left Oxford. Moore may not have known much about music, and what he did know he knew wrong; but Wilde knew nothing at all about this greatest of the arts.

* * *

Besides Moore, almost the only other person who roused Wilde to be scathing was a wealthy foreigner who had a house in London in which he received artists who had any claim to notoriety—actors and actresses, musicians and painters, as well as writers. I don't know at all what was the quarrel between him and Wilde, but it must have been very bitter. Wilde said of this man: "A. came to London with the intention of opening a salon and succeeded in opening a saloon."

One night he went into a fashionable restaurant with some friends, and when he was seated he glanced round the room and saw his enemy with a party at a near table. "I don't like that man's face," said Wilde in a loud voice. "Let us go somewhere else." And he got up and left the restaurant. After Wilde's imprisonment, this same man published a book in Paris, written in French, which was an indictment of Wilde, and, from that point of view, well done.

* * *

Still another enemy was Charles Brookfield, the actor, who used to boast, and with some reason, that he had done a great deal to bring about the downfall of Wilde. Brookfield was the son of a lady-in-waiting to Queen Victoria and of a royal chaplain. His family were those Brookfields whose name occurs so often in the letters of Thackeray. He was about the age of Wilde, having left Cambridge University nearly at the same time as Wilde left Oxford. I knew Brookfield, and liked him very much. In some respects I liked him better than I did Wilde. He was the most amusing of men, one who took responsibilities with a light heart—or rather met them by ignoring them; and he gave me the impression of having a loose grasp on realities. He wrote some plays which were trash to pass an evening, and a very good book of stories called *The Twilight of Love*, which ought to be reprinted, for these stories give a better picture of a certain kind of drink-and-women London life at the end of the last century than any book I know.

With Brookfield alas! Wilde became a monomania. There came a time when he could not keep Wilde out of his talk. I can only guess at the cause of this obsession. They had not been great friends and then quarrelled. Perhaps Brookfield grudged Wilde's success, thinking that while he had the same social talents as Wilde, he was rather in the lurch.

He wrote a burlesque which was played in London, called *Poets and Puppets*. In this Wilde was ridiculed as "O'Flahertie, a poet." Wilde did not seem to resent it, for he offered Brookfield parts in his plays; and Brookfield did play in *An Ideal Husband*. "I told him," said Brookfield, "that as I did not want to learn many of his lines I would take the smallest part, and I took the valet."

While this play was being prepared, Wilde insisted on a rehearsal on Christmas day, to the great disgust of the players. To make matters worse, he kept them waiting in a cold theatre for over an hour. When he did turn up, none of them, men or women, had the courage to tackle him except Brookfield:

"You don't keep Christmas, Oscar?"

"No, Brookfield, the only festival of the Church I keep is Septuagesima. Do you keep Septuagesima, Brookfield?"

"Well, no," said Brookfield. "Not since I was a boy."

When the scandal—the Queensberry scandal—broke out, Brookfield went about London, wherever he could go, organizing an opposition to Wilde. As he knew a vast number of people, and had a very persuasive speech, and a superb talent for ridicule, it is quite probable that he did considerably injure Wilde's cause.

I once heard Robert Ross complaining before Wilde, with much indignation, of Brookfield's activities. "How absurd of Brookfield!" said Oscar. That was all.

* * *

Certainly, Wilde was surprised at the storm of hatred and execration which struck him once he was down. He could not quite realize it. Himself so lacking in vindictiveness, so hard to stir to any inimical sentiment which went beyond a half-humorous dislike, he lent his own disposition in these matters to others. That the rage against him proceeded altogether, or even principally, from moral indignation, I don't believe for a moment.

I gathered from Guillaume Apollinaire, who reminded me in some ways of Wilde—he had the same facility, indolence, good-nature, and a like attraction for those who came within his rays—well, from him I gathered that he too was astonished at the animosity which declared against him when he was arrested and imprisoned on a stupid and false charge of being a party to a theft from the Louvre. A friend of his who telephoned to a man of some influence asking him to sign a petition to get Apollinaire out of prison, received this reply: "To get Apollinaire out of prison? Never. But I will sign a hundred petitions to keep him in prison." By the nature of things the volume of hatred which unfurled against Apollinaire was as a summer gale compared to the tempest which beat upon Wilde; for Wilde had an immense reputation, whereas Apollinaire was known only in Paris, and not widely known even there.

"So, to do justice to men," wrote the old seventeenth century Jansenist, Nicole, "we have only to know the laws of God, and keep them, and justice will follow of itself." But it was precisely some of those who prided themselves upon knowing and keeping the laws of God who were most cruel and unjust to Wilde.

VII

ALTHOUGH LEONARD SMITHERS, THE publisher, never came into Wilde's life till after Wilde's release from prison, he was such a permanent figure in it afterwards that some account must be given here of this curious man, the like of whom was never seen before in the fraternity of London publishers and doubtless will never be seen again.

He was a solicitor in Sheffield, and drifted into bookselling there to become the partner of one Nichols, who was, I think, his brother-in-law. Both came to London, but they quarrelled and separated, and lost sight of each other so completely that I had a letter from Nichols, written from New York during the Great War, to ask if I could give him any details of Smithers' end.

It was Arthur Symons who invented Smithers as the publisher of the new school of young poets and picture-artists. Among these there was henceforward a fissure, the more conservative remaining with John Lane, and Henry Harland and his subdued *Yellow Book*, as it was become after the expulsion of Aubrey Beardsley.

It is very remarkable how Smithers, who never became a Londoner, but always remained the provincial both in look and accent, whose previous life and training, it might be thought, would have induced him rather to fight shy of the ideals and notions and practices of his young clients (as in fact did his ex-partner Nichols), took to them, and not only that, but came to consider them his big business to the neglect of all else. He was a man whom at first sight you would have deemed insignificant. Pale hair, eyes which looked half at you and half somewhere else, a pasty white face, and the blanched hands which always seemed to need washing, or rather scrubbing to work up the circulation. On one of these hands was a large wedding-ring. How it had kept there was another miracle. He had been married twice. His two wives I knew, for he had kept on fair terms with the first, and whenever she came to London she would lunch or dine with him once or twice during her stay. Both wives were pretty women. The second Mrs. Smithers, she who shared the time of his glory, was rather full-bodied, high-coloured, with snapping black eyes and hair to match, and—yes, pretty. Very agreeable young woman too, always with the air of having been left at the half-way house and looking round for some passer to explain matters to her.

I was often in Smithers' company, in hers too, and liked them both very well. I believe that of all those he published, I was, with Beardsley and Dowson, the only one who had much liking for him. At this time he seemed about thirty-five years old, and his wife five or six years younger.

Symons thought to make him the Poulet-Malassis of London. Smithers, with his fiendish apprehensive qualities, at once adopted this suggestion, and set himself to learn all he could of this French publisher of the Second Empire who published Baudelaire, Champfleury, Soulary, Gautier, the engravers Rops and Méryon, and, under his hat, some things obscene and naïve—as obscene things always are in the publishing trade. It is only the police who take them seriously. Poulet-Malassis spent some time in gaol; Smithers never did, perhaps thanks to the good sense of the English police. Otherwise, one cannot but be struck by the resemblance between the life of Poulet-Malassis and his own.

Both flourished as booksellers who sell under the counter at artificial prices the absurd and ill-written pornography which no man or woman with some imagination wants to read; both had a middle time when they published poets, prose-writers, and pictorial artists of the highest value, a few of them men of genius without any doubt at all; and then both ended in obscurity, poverty, struggling to the last with their creditors.

Allowing for the essential and immense difference between a thorough Englishman and a thorough Frenchman, they must have had many traits in common. As is known, Baudelaire's *Les Paradis Artificiels* is an extension of De Quincey's *Opium Eater*, and when it was in the press Baudelaire had all the pains in the world to prevent Poulet-Malassis from inserting at the end of the book the advertisement of a dealer in drugs. Smithers would have done that too. Both again had spasmodic longings to publish a really notorious best-seller. Smithers used to think occasionally of opening negotiations with Marie Corelli, though he knew well enough that to publish one of her books would destroy the odd kind of distinction which clung about his name as a publisher, and has no doubt preserved it to this day.

Both Poulet-Malassis and Smithers had, I think, a happier life than if the one had stuck to the family printing-house at Alençon and the other to the family-solicitor's office at Sheffield, though their happiness was not of the kind which ropes in money. But is any man who ropes in money and pockets it so happy as he who squanders with one hand what he gains with the other?

Money, however, he must have had, and in considerable quantities sometimes, to judge by his migrations from a small room in a building off the Strand, Effingham House. "I'll publish anything that the others are afraid of," he said to me there the first day that Symons brought me to him with a book of very youthful stories, written to burlesque the variety of the Terror story then somewhat in fashion. He continued in that state of mind. His publication some few years later of *The Ballad of Reading Gaol* was the supreme demonstration of his attitude.

From one room in Effingham House to a shop in the Royal Arcade, where he had his glory, and thence to a shop in Bond Street, which was his field of Waterloo. For Smithers too inspired himself from Napoleon as from a brandy-bottle. He must at one time have given serious attention to Napoleon's career, for he seemed to know the Napoleonic bibliography pretty well and had always some interesting books on Napoleon and Josephine and Marie-Louise in his shop. Napoleon was the cocktail of the period.

For all the weight which a Bond Street address carries, Smithers' imprint on a title-page inspired little confidence and less respect.

Vincent O'Sullivan

In the newspaper offices they generally gave a Smithers' book to some young (or old) slugger to be cut up. He hardly ever advertised, preferring to circularise a list of possible purchasers, a method of trade carried over from the days when his principal stock was claustrated—just as he used occasionally to threaten to put a signboard in his Bond Street window bearing the words: "Smut is cheap to-day." And he was a man who would as soon have done it as said it, if pushed a little. The daily and weekly papers, therefore, had not to shew him or his team the consideration they kept for important advertisers. In a book of my own I had described a character as having "a fanatical nose." In one of the London papers, I forget the name, the title of the book was given, then the name of the publisher. Beneath, a single line: "What is a fanatical nose?" That was all the review.

If there were any variation in this haughty disdain, it was only to let the reviewer shew his infinite superiority and expand himself in abuse. Such was the fate often enough of Beardsley and of Arthur Symons and of some numbers of *The Savoy*. But generally, as for Ernest Dowson's beautiful poems, there was nothing but a sneer of neglect. My own little book of essays called *The Green Window* was given by some accident two full columns in *The Saturday Review*. But they were columns which no amount of self-flattery could persuade were complimentary. Smithers, however, was so unused to seeing anything about his books other than a little hole-and-corner notice, that he was as satisfied as a normal publisher might be if the long article had reeked with praise. What counted for him was that the article was *long*. He wanted to display the article in his window, but his lady-secretary, who was the tutelary angel for the time being, dissuaded him.

In considering Smithers as a publisher it must never be forgotten that during his few years of existence he produced some of the most beautiful books ever issued in any country. There were Beardsley's *Volpone, Mademoiselle de Maupin, Lysistrata, The Rape of the Lock,* and the chapters of his strange novel, *Under the Hill*. There were Conder's *La Fille aux yeux d'or* (Dowson's translation), Horton's *The Raven*, and *The Pit and the Pendulum* (my edition), Max Beerbohm's *Portraits of 25 Gentlemen*. And it should be said that the presentation of these books and of all his books was for the most part due to Smithers himself. Though he was surrounded by artists he did not seek their advice in such matters, or if he did, forgot it, or found some excuse to follow his own way. The little edition of *The Rape of the Lock*, which delighted Phil May, great artist too, but of course utterly different from Beardsley, was, I am sure, an idea of Smithers himself without any primary suggestion from Beardsley, who seemed to be satisfied to rest on the other edition—the large edition. *The Savoy* also, very original as to presentation, he was mostly responsible for himself, all but the name, which Beardsley took from the well-known London hotel.

Whatever may have happened to Smithers' authors (I am speaking of his good period, his Royal Arcade period), it would seem that his professional brethren, some of them at least, were not lacking in appreciation of his talent. One year, at the Publishers' (or was it Booksellers'?) dinner, Mr. Bernard Quaritch toasted Smithers as the cleverest publisher in London. This event had the effect of revealing the most unsuspected depths of natural simplicity in the astute and complicated man. Nothing else could have overwhelmed him to that extent, not even if he had been given a knighthood or elected Lord-Mayor, as such a tribute from one of the leaders of his trade; and this is curious, for he [was] always more an expensive bookseller and art-dealer than a publisher. He could not cease from talking about it. He had even trained the bountiful Alice (his wife) to keep the ball up, and when you met her it was: "Have you heard that at the Publishers' dinner Mr. Quaritch toasted Len as the," etc. etc.

But all that passed in trade circles and had no general effect on the reputation of his few authors. The "Smithers people" were always much disdained, not only in Fleet Street and thereabout, but in other latitudes—out there in Palace Court, for instance, where Alice Meynell in her soft precious voice, which large eyes, dark, protesting, sometimes passionate, accompanied dramatically, told us that Francis Thompson was *the* genius of the young generation. As for Aubrey Beardsley, dismissal with contempt—"one of the Smithers people." "He has a line in his hand," she remarked slightingly. I have often wondered what she meant.

Were we to judge of the intelligence of the English Press of the time by its reception of Beardsley, Symons, Dowson, and a few others, it would be impossible to put it very high. Oftenest there was not even a pretext of impartial judgment or of merely trying to understand. It was just welting and socks in the jaw. Still, it would be unjust to blame the English Press alone for ways which were followed elsewhere about the same time. In a lecture given not so long ago, Maeterlinck recalled to the audience that the reception of his plays by the French Press was a mixture of ridicule and contempt. The reception of *Pelléas et Mélisande*, he said, even with Debussy's music to support it, was something frightful. In Paris the Symbolists and a few of their elders, Mallarmé for instance, and Villiers de l'Isle-Adam, were figures of fun for the journalists.

But the young French poets hit back, and sometimes murderously, and they also had found a few defenders of weight, whereas in London the youthful "Smithers people" were as lambs led to the slaughter who opened not their mouths. The truth is that they were not given much opportunity to do so. The boasted "Fair Play" machinery was not in working order at the time—not, at any rate, where they were concerned.

I may give an instance from my own experience. The *Daily Chronicle* published a notice of a book of mine which must have had at the root of it some personal rancour either against the publisher or me, for all agreed that the book in itself was not enough to account for such an excess of venom. In reply to a letter I wrote him, the editor sent me a long communication in which, after unctuously remarking that they had been reluctantly obliged to treat me with more severity than the usual courtesy which distinguished their columns permitted, he acknowledged that I had some right to protest, and offered to publish my letter if I would soften it down according to a model which he inclosed. I could see that he was rather ashamed of the article, and sorry it had appeared, and at the same time wanted to cover his contributor; but as the reply he proposed to insert was faint and colourless, I refused to sign it, and no reply or defence or excuse of any kind was ever published by me or by anyone else.

* * *

In the Royal Arcade and Bond Street period of the Smithers epic, was also the house in Bedford Square. *Mansion* indeed is a more fitting word for it than house. I cannot think what Begum or else what profiteer by the Peninsular war had massed enough money to build it and enable the heirs to keep it up. I would sometimes go to see Smithers there at nightfall. A ring at the bell; and then again, and yet again, a ring. If it were a soft evening, the servants of the neighbouring houses taking the air against their employers' absence, would regard me disdainfully, ironically, and yet, as I was proud to discern, with some uneasiness. Ring. Ring again. And at last a slut—I beg her pardon, poor thing, wherever she is now—but that apron, those smudged cheeks, and that general suspicion and the hostility in her eyes which was as far as possible from the urbanity of the well-trained servant to the guest in a mansion in Bedford Square—well, a slut who said in an uncompromising tone: "'E said I wasn't to let no one in."

That barrier past, you followed the slut—a well-built girl who swayed her hips and shewed you what she was made of, holding your five bob (right of entry) tight in her hand—through huge high-ceilinged deserted rooms, ghost after ghost coming forth in the dim light to see who you were and whether by chance it might be one of *them* instead of Smithers you were come to visit.

But Smithers it was, and there he was at last, bending over a game of chess, often with Ernest Dowson, sometimes with Teixera de Mattos, sometimes with some man, or men, unknown, and Charles Conder coaching him.

There were never any of Smithers' women there. Or, at least, there was one, the one acceptable, the most sympathetic of Smithers' women. This was his wife, who was supposed to preside over the building—which it would have taken a Lady Castlereagh of the Pitt and Coburg era to preside over. There she was, not exactly in a corner, but looking as if she had been shoved aside into a corner and forgotten. I should have taken her for Welsh, but she had the same Sheffield accent as he had. Black hair, black eyes, smiling, florid, buxom and healthy, with full shoulders, breasts and arms, she was ready to talk really quite pleasantly of trivial things to any likely man who offered to pay some attention to the fact that she was there. My own belief is that she was faithful to Smithers, because, if for nothing else, he gave her a kind of exciting life she would never have had with any other man she might have met and married in Sheffield. Anyhow, faithful. Faithful against winds and tides, for she had all sorts of provocations; and he himself threw temptations in her way for the artistic pleasure of the spectacle. "She loves me," he would say with regret. Where she went to, or how she ended, I know not, but it can hardly have been by pleasant ways.

Once or twice I had reason to think that Smithers' attitude towards her was a bluff, and that he set more store on her than he would have us believe. One night in Brussels he invited myself and Beardsley, who was then living at an hotel in the rue Neuve and hating it, to the theatre de la Monnaie to hear *Carmen*. On this jaunt to Brussels he had quite exceptionally as his travelling companion Alice his wife, whom he generally left to amuse herself as best she could in London. That night Alice surpassed herself, shewing, like Madame de Staël, her advantages where she had them. And a man alone in a box, who looked an important personage, and perhaps was, fell for her with a thud.

I was sitting next to Alice and called her attention discreetly to her conquest. She played up in a way I should never have supposed she had it in her to do.

Afterwards, in a restaurant, there was the man again at an opposite table, and there was Alice too, and Smithers, who had at length become aware—he could scarcely help it—and who suddenly turned sarcastic and peevish.

How the comedy developed I do not know, for Beardsley in his half-invalid state had to go back to his hotel, and I went with him. The events that succeeded, as Smithers related them to me next day, were amusing enough, but cannot be printed. If what he said was true, cynicism in the manner of Dostoevsky had said its last word. But it is just as likely, and even more likely, that they left the restaurant soon after we did and returned to their hotel-room like a good bourgeois couple of moderate means and ideas as moderate.

* * *

For young men with endless hours on their hands, with no entry anywhere to employ their time, Smithers was the ideal publisher. He would sit in the Café Royal, or some other restaurant more or less near his place of business, through the long afternoons, with two or three of his young poets for company, discussing things the farthest removed from practical value. Sometimes his face would cloud. A figure had appeared in the doorway. This was a boy from his office hied to summon him to return to an appointment he could by no means shirk. Then he would rise slowly and heavily, hold out a flabby hand.

"What are you going to do?"

"I've got a vague idea I ought to do some work."

"Oh—Ah! All right! I'll be here at seven. Or at the Florence at half-past."

From time to time he would turn up in Paris, always accompanied by some appalling Venus—sagging breasts, pouched jaws, varicosed legs, rheumatic ankles, wall-eyed—hideous to the point that one wondered in what suburb of Houndsditch he could have gone to seek her. It was to one of these—they were never the same, yet all alike—that Wilde gave the answer reported by Frank Harris. She came from London with Smithers but she was a Belgian, and she spoke in French when she was presented to Wilde, "Monsieur Wilde, je suis la femme la plus laide de Londres." "Du monde, Madame, du monde," replied Wilde, with more truth and wit than grammar.

Smithers had never had anything but the petty sales, or the absence of sales, of his young men when, *The Ballad of Reading Gaol* having been refused by Lane and other publishers, Ross thought of Smithers. Smithers accepted as though it were a proposition to deal with an obscene book, and resorted to his usual furtive measures for a special kind of sale. The huge success of the poem took him entirely off his guard. He did not know how to handle a success of that kind; how to manage the advertising, the Press. It gave him ambition to launch out as a publisher, and when he got to Bond Street he published some incredible trash: he published anything offered to him if the writers would bear the expense; he even published a book called *Magister Adest*, written by a community of nuns—till he shut down altogether and disappeared. Thence from fall to fall to the end, and Lord Alfred Douglas paid his funeral expenses.

For his young poets he was, on the whole, a benediction. They would have been hard put to it to find another publisher in London. But he could be ferocious.

"What has brought you to Paris this time?"

"I've come to Paris to kill Dowson."

Poor Dowson, three-quarters dead already, and drifting round the Quartier Latin and the market-men's bars about the *Halles*, where he could drink all night. He did not much need the facilities which the momentary presence of Smithers had brought him, little able as he was to resist a possibility of endless drinking, endless souses from the fall of night. In his clearer moments he was translating for Smithers books considered then to be erotic—[Laclos'] *Les Liaisons Dangereuses*, Balzac's *La Fille aux yeux d'or*, this last with illustrations by Charles Conder. Smithers produced a very beautiful edition of Dowson's play *The Pierrot of the Minute*, and persuaded Beardsley, much against his will, to do pictures for it. "Dowson's filthy little play," said Beardsley—"filthy" to be taken here simply in the sense of bad as a play. He also got Beardsley to design the cover for Dowson's book of poems, and Beardsley did two curves, which, as he explained to me, represented the letter Y—"*Why* was this book ever written?"

This is not given as Beardsley's considered opinion about Dowson, and I don't believe it was. He would not have taken such pains with *The Pierrot of the Minute* if he had despised it altogether. He would not have done the pictures at all. Whatever Smithers may have thought of the rest of his young team, Beardsley he sincerely admired and, I think, under his cynical skin, even loved. I find it hard to imagine him forcing Beardsley to do anything which Beardsley did not want to do.

But in sight of Dowson's appearance and way of life, Beardsley lost all patience and tolerance, of which he had not a large stock. He knew he had only a few years to live, but he loved life, was interested in lots of things, was not in the least morbid, and if he had been able, would have taken part in all manifestations of life where were to be found brightness, music, comely women, beautiful dresses. The spectacle of a man slowly killing himself, not with radiance, still less with decorum, but in a mumped and sordid way, with no decoration in the process, but mean drinkshops, poisonous liquor, filth and malady, for all accompaniment to the march down under—that, when he saw it in Dowson, irritated Beardsley beyond control. Dowson's neglect of his personal appearance went to lengths which I have never seen in anybody else still on the surface, and hardly in bums and beats and down-and-out tramps forced by hardship to a condition which they have not the means to remedy. The thing about Dowson was that he did not want to remedy it. He was never denuded of money as Wilde was sometimes. But to spend money on baths and clothes and remedies seemed to him to be putting money to the wrong account. With Smithers, with myself, and, I suppose, with a few others, he used to go to very good and even fashionable restaurants. Although we did not escape attention, and no doubt suspicion, we heard no complaint. In the less urbane Paris of to-day we would be asked to go somewhere else.

Now that was just what Beardsley could not stand. He said it was unfair to bring a man like Dowson, who looked as if he had slept in the gutter and, what was more, had a very visible malady, among a number of well-dressed people who paid a good sum of money for the pleasure of dining in clean and wholesome surroundings. The few times he was inveigled by Smithers to spend an evening in Dowson's company he shewed his temper, fell into prolonged silences, and then would answer fretfully in retorts. One night at Bullier's, the students' dance-hall in the Quartier Latin, Dowson pointed out Julien Leclerq, a young poet, who was there dancing.

"He looks as if he had just stepped out of one of your pictures."

"Then the best thing he can do is to step in again," replied Beardsley, and went away on that.

When Beardsley read anything of Dowson's, the image of Dowson himself, with all there was in him to annoy and irritate, his gentle but terribly obstinate disputatiousness, came between the reader and the text. Owing to this he could never recognize in Dowson's writings their real value. If you tried to enforce upon him Dowson's artistic merits, you could not get far before he brought in the man.

"But Dowson is a great poet."

"I don't care. No man is great enough to excuse behaviour like his."

But even if Dowson had been personally all that Beardsley thought desirable, even if Beardsley had never seen him, he would hardly have cared much for the production of the poet. His taste, at least in English literature, was for the eighteenth century. Keats and Rossetti he professed to hate—though Wilde said that this was sheer perversity and an illustration of the truth that we often hate what is akin to us. Thackeray and Dickens did not really interest him at all, and Meredith only to a very limited extent. George Gissing was a novelist he loathed, and I never heard him speak well of Hardy. I never heard him speak well of any nineteenth-century English writer except Landor—a taste which there are few to share. He had by no means reached the epoch of permanent opinions or the summit of his powers. He was still in what is called a state of becoming when he died at twenty-five.

As for Dowson, I have read here and there that Smithers was responsible for his squalor and degradation. This charge should be put aside. Without pretending that Smithers was adorned with "the white flower of a blameless life," it may safely be assumed that for Dowson he was, on the whole, a benefit. It was he who provided Dowson with his principal means of subsistence for a period covering some years. If his remittances in the last months of the poet's life fell off or ceased (I don't know that they did), it should be remembered that about this time he was plunged in difficulties himself.

Dowson liked Smithers, and he might well, for Smithers seemed to do everything he wanted. Smithers at times spoke scandalously of Dowson, as at times he spoke scandalously of everybody except Aubrey Beardsley; but all the verse or prose Dowson cared to produce, Smithers was ready to publish. Smithers, and no one else in London. Some years after the poet's death another publisher issued a volume which contained the two Smithers volumes, but with the Dedications suppressed, and, I think, another arrangement in the placing of the poems. But during Dowson's lifetime nobody but Smithers would look at him. As Dowson became unwilling or unable to produce original work, Smithers put him on translations. I believe that some of Dowson's friends took objection to that, saying that Smithers, by giving Dowson sweating wages to translate dirty French books, prevented the poet from continuing with his own genius.

Balzac's book and the book of Choderlos de Laclos, [who was] the general of the Convention and the Consulate, which are the two books Dowson translated for Smithers, are generally considered as masterpieces. That unscrupulous dealers in Paris and elsewhere sell Dowson's translations for much money to travellers from the Antipodes and the United States as "racy French girl-stories" does not affect the matter; and, indeed, one might paraphrase Dr. Johnson's saying about *Clarissa Harlowe* and say that a man who should read these books to find indecencies would hang himself. If Baudelaire offered to prepare a critical edition of *Les Liaisons Dangereuses* for Poulet-Malassis, it is hard to see Dowson as a degraded hack because he translated the same book for Smithers. And Dowson himself was very far from considering himself degraded by the kind of work upon which Smithers employed him. What he disliked was the work, not the nature of the work.

With about as much plausibility, Smithers has been also accused of hastening Dowson's end by associating with the poet in his debauches. Dowson's relations with Smithers lasted about four years. During this space of time Dowson was not very much in London or for long at a time, his love affair with the Italian restaurant-keeper's daughter having arrived at the dead point where there was no hope left. He was a year in Brittany, where Smithers never went near him. He was also for a long spell in Paris. If Smithers did go to see him while he was in Brittany—but I feel sure he did not—there was not much material for debauch to be found in a little Breton town, unless one were as those heroes of Villiers de l'Isle-Adam who, when they went to England, would squander millions recklessly in the gaming-halls and bordelloes of Canterbury or Bury Saint Edmunds. Smithers went from time to time to Paris, and also to Brussels, which he liked more than Paris, but his absence from England never lasted more than four or five days. Hence his occasions were limited for persuading Dowson to a life of debauchery. Besides, if he had been St. Francis de Sales and John Wesley rolled together instead of the man he was, he would not have succeeded in prevailing upon Dowson to see any charm in a sober, godly and tranquil life.

That Dowson was in rather poor health was pretty evident all the time I knew him, but not that he was in a desperate condition. In the letter which Smithers wrote me at the time of the poet's death there was sorrow and also surprise. Certainly he had not realized that Dowson was so near his end.

When I told him that Jean de Tinan, a young man well known at the time, a friend of mine, but not of Smithers, was dead at twenty-three, he asked me of what ill did he die. Then said I: "The doctors declared he was worn out by the life he had led." Smithers laughed sardonically. "Damned puny Frenchmen! They can't stand anything. Look at Dowson. Is he dead? Is Conder dead? Am I dead?"

"No," I might have answered to all three questions, "but pretty near." But I did not think that at the time, and I must have agreed with Smithers, considering it one of his side-kicks at the men he paid. Dowson was one. Conder was another. Conder arrived at the Royal Arcade one fine morning in May and told Smithers that he wanted to go to Brittany "to paint blossom." "There was a man waiting for him outside," said Smithers, "who, I believe, was Dowson." He ended by paying for the journey to Brittany and went over later to join them in Paris or Brussels.

One night, just after he had published *The Ballad*, in a club near Whitehall he fell into a dispute with a man who had been a friend of Wilde's, and had recently published a life of Victor Hugo, I think. The man spoke disparagingly of Wilde's poem and seemed to blame Smithers for publishing it.

"I don't think you are at your best," quoth Smithers perfidiously, "in that Life of Victor Hugo. It doesn't seem to be *you*."

"It's me at a hundred pounds," replied the man. "If you want the frills you must pay for them."

About a book of mine which he had in hand I was very uncertain, and one day I mentioned to Smithers that it might be advisable to shew the MS. to Arthur Symons.

"What good can it do you to have the opinion of somebody no better than yourself?" said Smithers brusquely.

I had my own share of conceit, but all the same, I was taken aback. Think of it! Smithers thought me as good as the great Symons, editor of *The Savoy*, contributor to *The Saturday Review* and other weeklies which would have declined contemptuously even a letter from me. I thought Smithers sincere, and I think so still, though his sincerity may have been only momentary, for he would blow from east and west within a few hours. Anyhow, nobody else spoke to me like that, and so I keep my regard for him, no matter what the excavators may have turned up, or will turn up in the future, in his letters against me. Besides, I don't care what he may have said. He was often half-drunk in his later phases, and also poisoned by the drugs which he was continually taking to prop up his shattered health.

So far as I can say, he never exploited any of those who worked for him. However, I recall that one night in a London music hall, while the performance was in full swing, at a little corner bar on the promenade, the barmaid and I assisted, silent and aghast, at a battle between Symons and Smithers about some matter of which I knew as little as the barmaid. That was not an Arthur Symons that I, or probably Smithers, had ever seen before. Instead of the ever-smiling and amiable young man full of engaging anecdotes of his friends among the ballet-girls, here was an unrelenting requisitor, battering down, it was only too easy to see, all the defences of the demoralized Smithers. Finally Symons went away—"I will say good-night to *you*, O'Sullivan"—

leaving Smithers "groggy." "Whoever would have thought it to look at him!" he groaned, wiping the sweat from his face. "Iron painted to look like a lath," I—or the barmaid—murmured to soothe him.

I said to him one day that as there were among those he had published two or three who were bound to survive, he would go down to posterity with them. He shook his head. "If the publisher is remembered at all, he is never remembered well."

And, as a fact, Smithers seems to be remembered, but remembered in a bad sense. That is not just: he was worth more than that.

VIII

To examine the metaphysics of Wilde's aesthetic theory, to trace the many influences so well assimilated, to disengage what really is original—not very much, but still distinctly there—is what I do not propose to do, for it would require as many pages again as I have written. His doctrine was conveyed by implication rather than by assertion: the very title of the book which chiefly contains it, *Intentions* [published in 1891], and the dialogue form, shew that he did not wish to be absolute. If he had been put to it, he would doubtless have agreed that few things are certain enough to be positive about.

* * *

Among the influences, Pater need be no more than mentioned. Wilde took the philosophy of the Oxford recluse, refashioned it, drew from it inferences which seem to go beyond the thought of the original, and brought it in an accessible, lively, and much commoner form to the ken of the general reader, who had been profoundly indifferent to this philosophy while it lay between the covers of *The Renaissance* and *Marius*. Pater took a "save me from my friends" attitude, and wrote certain guarded things which were meant as a disavowal of Wilde's interpretation of his work. "The strange vulgarity which Mr. Wilde mistakes for cleverness," he brought himself to say in one of his less prudent moments.

* * *

The influence of Ruskin is far less explicit in Wilde's essays and lectures, but implicitly it is very observable. He told me that when he was a very young man the two men he desired most to know were Pater and Ruskin. Ruskin has been, since his death, in a tunnel, from which he now at last seems to be emerging. The young men of the eighteen-nineties had not words bad enough for Ruskin. Wilde, who belonged to an earlier generation, kept all his respect for Ruskin; but he was very discreet about it, unless he happened to be talking with somebody who admired Ruskin, such as myself.

Ruskin's passion for mingling considerations of British Protestantism with judgments on Florentine and Venetian art, and on art generally, his Victorian sentimentalizing over the "workman" (though it can hardly be called Victorian, since Lamennais, and many others under his direction, among them George Sand, were doing the same thing in France)—all that part of Ruskin, Wilde neglected. He also seemed to neglect Ruskin's political economy, though in his great essay *The Soul of Man*, there are traces of it. After being jeered at unmercifully, Ruskin's political economy is now considered worthy of some attention. Where Wilde found his particular Ruskin, as Marcel Proust was to do later, was in *The Bible of Amiens*, *Sesame and Lilies*, *The Crown of Wild Olive*, in parts of *Mornings in Florence* and *St. Mark's Rest* and of *Modern Painters*. He accepted Ruskin on the Pre-Raphaelites. How far he accepted Ruskin's opinion of Turner I don't know; but Turner is surely a great painter, one of the greatest of the English, one of the greatest of all modern painters, and Ruskin was certainly justified in all he said of him.

Wilde had many stories about Ruskin. One of them has a little of the charm which all those who knew Ruskin seem to have found in him. He had Ruskin as his guest at dinner in some restaurant or club. He asked Ruskin what wine he would like. Ruskin answered that he had given up wine; it was not a necessity.

"But as a luxury, Mr. Ruskin?"

Ruskin thought a moment: "Well, then, as a luxury—and let it be a large one."

* * *

Others of his more or less contemporaries whom he was willing to speak of very fully and with admiration were Carlyle and Rossetti. I suppose Matthew Arnold must have been still another, seeing the marked influence of Arnold on some of his poems; but, personally, I never heard him talk with any enthusiasm of Arnold, and all I recall of what he said of Arnold is that he once urged him to write more poetry. Arnold replied: "When I wrote poetry people told me I ought to write prose. Now that I write prose they tell me I ought to write poetry." Wilde's opinion seemed to be that Arnold had too much of the Oxford Don. He professed a dislike of the University Don manner. "One cannot live at Oxford because of the Dons."

* * *

He had, as is well known, academic successes at Trinity College, Dublin, and at Oxford, but he drew no pride from them, and never spoke of them to me or, I should think, to anyone. I had an amusing enough instance of his indifference to his scholastic prowess. After his condemnation, his house was pillaged in a disgraceful fashion by his creditors. So extraordinary was the state of men's minds in England at that time, that the inviolability of the private house, which the English make so much of, in Wilde's case became a dead letter. No attempt seemed to be made to protect anything of Wilde's. After a little, things of his, some of them very private things, began to appear in shops in Chelsea and in streets near the Strand. As I found it rather painful to see such things, some of them, as I say, very personal, put up for sale without the owner's consent, I bought up several of them, intending to return them to Wilde. This I did. He accepted all except one. It was a history of English literature in two volumes which had been given to him as a prize at his Irish School—the Enniskillen school, as well as I remember—and the arms of the school were stamped in gilt on the cover, and there was a laudatory inscription.

Wilde looked at the volumes with a sort of horror and then began to laugh.

"However could you imagine! Do take those dreadful things away. Don't keep them yourself. Give them to the cab-driver."

* * *

Among the things in his house which were pillaged was Carlyle's writing-table. That bears testimony to his admiration of Carlyle. Wilde is now often associated with the young men of the eighteen-nineties, but, as I have said, many of his admirations were not shared by them. Did the young men of the period admire Sarah Bernhardt and Henry Irving as Wilde did? Some of them, perhaps—I think Symons was one. But Beardsley, to take the excelling genius of that time, among French actresses preferred Réjane—her face appears in several of his drawings—and among English, a music-hall singer named Marie Lloyd. I once told Beardsley that Wilde had given me a discourse on Carlyle's *French Revolution*, beginning with the flight of "the unclean thing," Madame Dubarry.

"What unclean thing?" said Beardsley. "How was she unclean? She was perfectly charming. That kind of twaddle makes me seasick. And it is so like Oscar."

But Wilde was simply representing the puritan Carlyle, and had not quite adopted his opinion about Madame Dubarry. In fact, he explained some of Carlyle's prejudices by—well, let us say that Carlyle would have been an unsatisfactory lover for Madame Dubarry. Wilde considered Carlyle's *French Revolution* as the work of a great artist, whatever its value as history.

* * *

Among his foreign admirations there was Flaubert, of course, and also Anatole France. One would have thought that Goethe would have been among the number, but so far as I know, he was not much interested in Goethe. One day while on a favourite topic, Napoleon, he repeated the Emperor's well-known remark after his interview with the German poet: "*There* is a man." "The story is incomplete," observed Wilde. "Goethe, on his side, must have said: "*There* is a poet.'"

* * *

His interest in foreign literature was practically confined to France. He did not care about Germany, gave no attention to its art, and knew nothing about it. He went even so far as to deny that any art was to be found there.

Nietzsche and Ibsen had become known in England and France while Wilde was in his productive state; but there is not the slightest sign of their influence on his work. Nietzsche perhaps he did not know; what he knew of Ibsen he disliked. To the Russians also he seemed indifferent.

And yet it was in Northern Europe, in Scandinavia and also in Russia, but especially in Germany, that his posthumous fame began. It is possible that to others he may have shewn more interest in Ibsen and the Russian novelists. I can only speak from my own experience. His books and plays are there for all to see, and his was a kind of talent that shewed the marks of whatever profoundly moved him. The modern German play-writers and novelists were not even names to him, and the modern Italians, D'Annunzio, for instance, little more than names. As for the United States, he shared Matthew Arnold's views on the kind of civilization, or lack of civilization, which he thought prevailed there, and its literature he did not take seriously except in Poe and Whitman and Hawthorne, not really liking any of them, I think, but Hawthorne—the Hawthorne of *The Scarlet Letter*. He once spoke of an American named Edgar Saltus whom he had known through Stuart Merrill. He had read one of his books (*Tristram*— something or other) and liked the plot. "But all that is related in the style of *A Painful Accident in New Jersey.*" I asked him if he had read anything of Julian Hawthorne. He said he had read one or two novels, and when I said that I thought Julian superior in many ways to his father he seemed to agree.

* * *

He submitted to certain influences, not from lack of funds of his own, but from admiration, of which he had a large stock. When all has been said about these influences, it must be recognized that in the main he composed himself. There has never been anybody like Oscar Wilde. All due allowance having been made for the influence of Flaubert on *Salome*, it remains as essentially Oscar Wilde as the opera-music which Richard Strauss composed for it is essentially Richard Strauss.

As for the influence of Huysmans on *Dorian Gray*, it is hardly worth mentioning. It does not affect the main part of the book, and in the chapter where it does, it would never occur to anyone that *À Rebours* had any influence on the writing if Wilde himself had not spoken of this in cross-examination by a lawyer.

And his wit and humour, of so very special a kind that it can easily be distinguished from any other, from whom did he derive that? Surely not from any of those he considered the masters of his youth. Pater and Ruskin were devoid of humour. Rossetti, it seems, had at one time that propensity to jokes at the expense of other people found in medical and art students—the most gloomy form of the comic. Carlyle had a sardonic humour which was highly unpleasant for the person it was exercised upon. None of them had the lightness, the gaiety or, above all, the good-humour of Wilde. He was not afraid to strike, but he was unwilling to wound. He had to have the strongest reasons for disliking a man to say anything harsh about him. Questions he considered excessive or impertinent he put aside disdainfully under the mask of humour. Thus, to someone who asked him if he never took any exercise, he answered lightly: "I believe I once played a game of dominoes outside a café."

* * *

It is to this good-humour, this consideration for the feelings of others, however young and insignificant, that one always comes back in thinking of Wilde's talk. There was nothing trenchant about it, no air of laying down the law without privilege of appeal, of uttering truths indisputable and not to be disputed. Some writers I have known and the most barren, gave the impression in their conversation that they were afraid to let themselves go lest their hearer should steal some of the mediocre notions they might emit, or that they might lose something which they could more profitably put in their books. There was not a sign of that in Wilde, because, as I have said, he liked much better to talk than to write.

At times his talk was a monologue, but generally it was real talk. He watched his listener closely, waited for his replies, studied his mood and adapted himself to it. There, no doubt, was the weakness of Wilde's talk: it lay in his pliancy, his readiness to swerve round. One day when he was talking with vast enthusiasm of Rossetti, I threw something disparaging across his path—from sheer perversity it must have been, for even now I have great admiration for Rossetti, and at that time I had more. Wilde stopped dead; I could see that he did not like what I had said; but in a moment he had brought his mind round to a new position and was developing brilliant variations on the theme that Rossetti was a foreigner and did not know the English language.

There were some astute men, enemies of Wilde, who used to say that he could only talk to women and young men, and avoided those who were his intellectual equals or superiors—that is to say, themselves. The truth is that there was a certain description of man loathed by Wilde. This was the kind of man who insists on precise facts in the most casual of talks. Thus, if Wilde, sailing along beautifully, should happen to say: "On the morning of the fifteenth of June, Napoleon, seeing that Grouchy did not come up, and that all was lost—," some man might pop his head out and declare in a tone which brooked no denial: "You are wrong, Oscar. It was the eighteenth of June, and the time was three o'clock in the afternoon." That kind of thing really had the power of exasperating Wilde beyond endurance. He said freely that he abhorred such men; but that is not a proof that he regarded them as his intellectual superiors, or even as his equals, or that they were.

There were, of course, men in the England of his time, of his own age, men very well known, who were his intellectual superiors; and he knew some of them. I never heard that any of these men denied that he was superior to them all as a talker. In France, though he spoke the language easily, he spoke it faultily, and with a strong English accent; yet all the men and women he met in France worth considering came under his charm, and this in the country the least patient with those who do not speak its language well.

As he lay dying, a friend of his, known in London for his witty sayings, came over to see him, and was sitting with him one afternoon. Wilde awoke from a doze and said: "I have had an appalling dream. I dreamed I was banqueting with the dead."

"My dear Oscar," replied the other cheerfully, "I am sure you were the life and soul of the party."

And that was just it.

IX

Unlike certain writers, known to us all, who seem always to be aiming at "Men's business and bosoms" though never quite arriving there, the human, and still more the humanitarian, element is practically lacking in Wilde's books. In personal intercourse he shewed himself interested in all varieties of human nature. It went even to domestic details. At Dieppe an Englishwoman invited him to luncheon, and took occasion to praise her claret, which, she said, good as it was, she had bought for a ridiculously low price—a franc, or something, a bottle. Wilde deliberately sipped the wine, put down his glass, and said gently: "They overcharged you."

* * *

Many will be surprised, and he himself would perhaps have been annoyed to hear that he struck me, at least, as a thoroughly well-organized person with a strong dose of common-sense. His advice in practical matters was sound, as Wordsworth's and Browning's is said to have been. What was striking about him came from the emanation of his personality working by its natural law; eccentricities he had none. Eccentricity is by no means, as people think, always artificial and a "pose"; it is the expression of a personality which does not take account of contingencies. When Wagner used to walk about the streets of Vienna flourishing a red handkerchief and talking to himself, he was certainly not aware that he was doing anything unusual. The long hair, the strange garb, and the lily and sunflower of Wilde's youth were theatrical and deliberate. In his later years the only thing which struck one as out of the way in his dress were the curious rings he wore. His clothes were of the kind worn by the usual Englishman; but the best tailor in London could not have made Wilde look well dressed. He had neither the build, nor the knack of wearing clothes, to appear the dandy he aspired to be. He was not "quiet" enough; there was, as I have already explained, something excessive about his appearance, such as is now and then seen in actors.

* * *

In build he was very tall and, for all the time I knew him, massive. With regard to this, there is in a *Life of Lord Carson* a very ridiculous anecdote. It will be remembered that Carson was the lawyer opposed to Wilde in the Queensberry trial. Some time after Wilde came out of prison, Carson, it seems, happened to be in Paris. One day at a street crossing he stepped back abruptly to avoid the traffic and in so doing bumped against a man just behind him who reeled from the shock and nearly fell. Carson looked closely at "the poor painted creature" (*sic*) and saw it was Wilde.

The only thing against this pretty dramatic story is that it relates a physical impossibility. Carson was a tall thin man who weighed many pounds less than Wilde. When a bicycle and a motor-car collide it is not the motor-car that topples over. After that, it is needless to add that Wilde never put paint on his face, or anything else but soap and water.

He was not what could be called a handsome man. He had not a single good feature; but his face taken altogether was unusual and striking. His hands were ugly, and as he employed them much while talking, waving them, cigarette between the fingers, with slow episcopal gestures, it was impossible not to remark their uncouthness. His eyes were large, blue or grey-blue, and rather protruding under heavy lids. I never saw in them that expression of haze and dreaminess which has been reported of some geniuses; but at times they took on a look often found in the eyes of sailors and aviators—a looking out, a looking beyond, a stare that would penetrate to the invisible. Before his imprisonment he wore his hair in the fluffy way, artificially waved, seen in his photographs. Afterwards, he brushed it back from his forehead, with great advantage to his appearance, for thus was brought out the real power which lay in his face and which is not expressed in any portrait of him I have seen. All these give him too soft a look. Some do not resemble him in the least. Among these is Toulouse-Lautrec's pastel, which has, however, value as evidence of Wilde's celebrity in Paris before his imprisonment—a fact rather doubted by some recent French writers. But Toulouse-Lautrec was not the kind of artist who does portraits "on commission." A man or woman had to be famous or notorious before he troubled about them.

Wilde's face in his later years was of the heavy type—rather an eighteenth-century face.

* * *

There is a portrait of George Sand which surely gives a better notion of what Wilde must have been as a young man than any of his own portraits. Sand in this portrait is wearing a man's coat, her hair is short for a woman of her time, and the general expression is masculine. It might pass for a portrait of a man of thirty, it might pass for a portrait of Wilde at about the same age. He must have looked like that at thirty.

It is not hard to find resemblance other than physical between the two. Wilde described himself as "a lord of language"; she was a lady of language. Sheer verbalism was the snare of them both. In Sand it took the form of sterile declamation, and in Wilde of oppressive decoration, and also, in parts of his plays, of declamation. Anybody who will look at some of Sand's plays will see a considerable resemblance in method, and even in other things, to those of Wilde. Sand's work is now, apart from her memoirs and letters, mostly unreadable, and she herself hardly lives save by two of the men who were her lovers, little as she anticipated any such outcome. Wilde's books have to-day considerable vogue; but then, for years after her death Sand's books too were vital in Europe. As an artist, Wilde is superior to Sand in knowing how to present and what to leave out. Here Wilde's indolence stood him in good stead against Sand's industry, which was like that of Anthony Trollope and had the same plethoric results. But whatever her failures or her faults as an artist, Sand in her best moments is a great romantic writer, often better than Wilde so far as the actual writing goes.

Other resemblances of a more personal nature may be indicated. Both had a propensity to call down a sort of Nestorian Christ and to implicate him in their affairs. At times they identified themselves with this Christ. George Sand was by far the most extravagant in this respect; her Christ was summoned to witness the dramas of her bedroom.

"But to whom shall I say all that? To you, walls of my cell which echo the moaning of my heart? To you, terrible skull full of a poison more deadly than those which kill the body, coffin in which I have laid my final hope? Or to you, O silent and unhearkening Christ? Still, whatever words I may say, however sobs may tear my breast, I know well that it is you, and only you, who will pardon. Begin by giving forgetfulness and repose to this heart devoured by grief; for while I thus suffer and love, I know that your anger will endure. O Christ, sublime man, to whom shall ever rise the plaint of hapless mankind, O my brother, though you are supreme and I am but as a little child, yet have I understood your soul, and by you have I been saved. Like you, it was good for me to have suffered, and my torments have not been in vain."

That happens to be George Sand, but it might very well be Oscar Wilde in his later manner.

They were both in full possession of their physical powers and perfectly capable of dealing with the world. Shyness could never have troubled either of them, or an even momentary lack of the skill to put their best foot foremost. A certain man, a publisher, lately spoke of some dealings he had with Villiers de l'Isle-Adam, a genius who touched summits which neither Sand nor Wilde ever came near. Now from the way this man spoke of Villiers and of the few wretched francs he had paid for *L'Eve Future*, it was quite evident that he had no sort of idea of the value of the man he had seen before him. But Buloz was not allowed to make any mistake about the value of George Sand, or John Lane, or any other London publisher, about the value of Wilde.

Further, they were both generous, teeming with ideas which they scattered about recklessly—Sand, who was not considered by the wits a good talker, in letters, and Wilde in talk, and also in letters. Sand has been called vulgar compared to Alfred de Musset, as Wilde has been called vulgar compared to Pater; but she undoubtedly supplied Musset, perhaps more than anybody knows, with ideas which he was not above adopting. There are passages in his works which are taken from her letters to him almost word for word. Both of them were generous too with money. "The only good of making money is the pleasure of spending it." That again happens to be George Sand, but it might be Oscar Wilde. I would not push the parallel too far. I offer it as curious, seeing the marked facial resemblance between the two. Wilde was not a hypocrite and George Sand was a shocking one. And if Sand had a sense of humour up to about forty, she lost it entirely after that age. It had always been liable to prolonged eclipses. That a woman who had admitted all Europe to the incontinence of her life, who had written to Sainte-Beuve that all she cared about was that people should not say that she received two men in her bed in the same day, should some years later turn Chopin out of her house at Nohant, and give as a reason for this break that her dignity as a mother would suffer if he remained under her roof, whatever else it shews, shews an appalling lack of humour.

If Wilde died too soon, George Sand died too late. For her fame, she ought to have died at the Chartreuse de Valdamosa, on the Spanish island, in the first of her years with Chopin. By that time she had written most of what is best in the vast extent of her work; she was still free-handed, good-humoured, good-natured, and she had not yet taken it into her head that she was a moral power, nor definitely turned preacher. If instead of writing moralizing and often tedious stories, she had found the courage to express herself, with her gift of writing, her admirable style, she would have been among the most memorable, and far greater than Wilde. She would have become a great heroine of sentiment, and sentimental pilgrims would to this day carry flowers to her grave.

But, as it was, she had no tragedy. She had only the tragedies of others. As she was the cause of those tragedies, she tried to see them as her own, and herself as the victim. So the proverbial tardy justice has taken a hand, and it is from the side of those who provided her tragedy and suffered it that vengeance has fallen on George Sand.

* * *

But Wilde, alas! had his tragedy.

At Naples one night we had sat late in a restaurant. It was the first night of a new play in the theatre which was hard by. About half-past eleven the restaurant was invaded by a fashionable crowd who shewed a great interest in Wilde's presence, and those who knew him by sight began pointing him out to others. To me it seemed just barefaced curiosity, inconsiderate but not insolent, and not hostile. Wilde, however, was profoundly disturbed. He seemed to strangle. "Let us go," he said, in a thick voice.

Outside, the city lay quiet and strange under the moon. We went a little way in silence. Then one of those tragic beggars of Naples arose in a doorway where he had been crouching and held out his hand. Wilde gave him money, and I heard him murmur in English: "You wretched man, why do you beg when pity is dead?"

From that hour I felt that the inexorable curtain had begun to fall and that Oscar Wilde had lived.

X

This same George Sand, a year or so after Balzac's death, wrote what follows:

> To say of a man of genius that he was essentially kind-hearted is the highest praise I know. Every exceptional character has to contend with so many obstacles and sufferings that the man who works out the mission of his talent with patience and good-humour is a great man, in every sense of the term. Patience and good-humour are strength; no man was ever stronger than Balzac. I have continually seen him the victim of great injustice, whether literary or personal; I have never heard him say a bad word of anybody. With a smile in his soul he carried through his painful life to the end. Full of himself, passionately interested in his art, he was really modest in his way, beneath his air of vanity and self-assurance, which was simply the *naïveté* of the artist. For great artists are always children.

This, of course, is rather idealized as applied to Balzac, who said and wrote many "bad words" about Sainte-Beuve, and lampooned George Sand's erewhile friend, Mme. d'Agoult. But it might go as the last word on Wilde with hardly any alteration. At one of the interminable trials which followed one another for years after his death in the English law-courts, the judge remarked: "Oscar Wilde was a very bad man." Well, all the stultifying poisonous vices he was without. He had no rancour. He was generous of everything he possessed—ideas, money, time. His temper he never allowed to get the better of him. I doubt if he had in his composition that ghastly white temper which is like madness. The most he ever showed was a flustered sort of indignation which was soon appeased.

I said to him one day: "I am glad to find you in Paris. I read in the French papers that you were in Constantinople."

He replied: "The French papers are delightful. They print the most absurd things about me."

But they printed, some of them, scandalous insults too, as he knew quite well.

* * *

Princess Belgiojoso, a woman very well known in French society during the Second Empire, made a point of communicating at the twelve o'clock mass at the Madeleine, a mass at which nobody communicates. She would march up to the sanctuary rail, the mass would stop, and the priest would be obliged to come down from the altar. Sainte-Beuve considered such conduct disgusting and made some scathing remarks about the Princess. Wilde, when I spoke of this, was more indulgent. He thought the Princess did right to have a private interview with God.

I can only speak for myself. I have always known better what I don't like than what I like. Certainly I have known people I have liked better than I did Wilde. But never one it was such a happiness to see or be going to see. It was rather like the emotion of going to hear some Schubert music, some Schumann, well sung, well played. You never felt that he cared very much for you, but you felt that he was glad to see you then and there. Some who saw him oftener and for long spells together may have found him otherwise. One or two, by their accounts, evidently did. But even they, putting things at their worst, do not seriously alter the features of his good-natured character.

He was good-natured, kind-hearted, but not large-hearted. He probably never cared for anyone as much as some cared for him. Lord Alfred Douglas essentially and practically far kinder to Wilde than Wilde ever was to Douglas. This was Lionel Johnson's opinion too, and he was a friend of Douglas (they had been at Winchester School together), and an acquaintance of Wilde. He expressed his view in a sonnet, which may be found among his poems, addressed to Wilde, although he is not named. The first line of the sonnet is:

> I hate you with a necessary hate.

* * *

Vincent O'Sullivan

The opinion sometimes put forward that Wilde was a weak, flabby person, victimized by his friends, should be abandoned. He was just the contrary: he was a force. Nobody in the wide world could persuade him to do what he did not want to do. If his friends were not his victims, except in the sense that he brought bad luck,[5] he was certainly not the victim of his friends. There be some—Marcel Proust was one—who throw themselves open-breasted on friendship. Sometimes it is on lances they throw themselves. But Wilde was not that kind of being. To hear him say: "So-and-so is a great friend of mine," you had the impression that he liked "So-and-so" as he liked a bottle of champagne. Sometimes a slight contempt entered into it, as when he said of Stuart Merrill, who was devoted to him, though he refused to see him in his last years: "I saw Stuart in the street the other day. He looked fat and married." The fine flower and culmination of the Wilde doctrine of friendship is André Gide, who is surely not the victim of anyone, not even of himself. But one knows that Gide's friendship for Wilde could not survive seeing in a café a man on whom sorrow and disgrace had fallen and also poverty. There is nothing crueller than Gide's account of his last interview with Oscar Wilde.

* * *

Considerable strength of character and social virtues were required for a man like Wilde to assume the position he did in English society, not simply among fine people, but among people in general. He had no family connexions, no politics to help him, yet he was far better known to the crowd than many who had.

---

5 The notion that he brought bad luck was held by several. Beardsley had it so strongly that he would not keep even a book of Wilde's by him. None of those among his close friends seems to have had a fortunate life. Equally strange, and remarked by himself, is the fact that many of those who were most active to compass his ruin, either died within a few years after he was cast into prison, or fell on misfortune in one shape or other.

Since the Great War a career like Wilde's has become easier with the fall of all sorts of prejudices; and still no figure anything at all comparable to Wilde's in dominance has appeared in England. There are a number of men who are famous in their line, but that is where they differ from Wilde, who was not famous in any line, but as a man. It cannot be said that he was famous by his books, for he was famous long before he wrote *Dorian Gray* and his plays. His earlier books never reached the public.

Some who have written on Wilde conclude that he owed his vogue in England to his plays. Another, one of your junior Frenchmen, will have it that he was simply a grotesque, a kind of buffoon, who attracted people like a circus or a street-juggler does. At his best, *a boulevardier* like that *Milord Arsouille* who was a by-word in Paris. Still another, that he was incapable of any serious intellectual effort, and that he never wrote *Salome* at all, which was for the most part the work of young Frenchmen, friends of Wilde.

Between the *boulevardier* of the second Empire, a type which endured in declining phases till the present century was well begun, between the position of men such as Catulle Mendès, Barbey d'Aurevilly, and some others, and the position of Wilde, there was the same difference as between the Paris of Offenbach and the London of Queen Victoria. Wilde's career at its summit, that is, in the eighteen-eighties—for as a social value he had begun to decline some few years before the crash in 1895—was on a much higher and more brilliant scale than that of any Parisian *boulevardier* of the same epoch. As to *Salome*, none of the young French writers who made verbal corrections in the text—Marcel Schwob, Pierre Louÿs, Stuart Merrill—could have written it, any more than they could have written the opera of Richard Strauss. They might perhaps have written something better, but they could not have written a thing so characteristically Oscar Wilde. One of these young men, Merrill, told me with much amusement that Wilde, resenting some of Merrill's suggestions as to grammar and phrasing, put them loftily aside, saying that Merrill was a foreigner and did not know French—Merrill being by origin an American.

The position he had in London he owed to personal and social qualities, not to anything he wrote, and certainly not to his plays, which came late in his career. By the first of them, *Lady Windermere's Fan*, Wilde did not become known to the English public; on the contrary, people went to see it because it was by Wilde. He is now thought of as a writer, as a poet; but at the time of his first play he was so little the professional writer that he paid for the publication of it himself. In the eighteen-eighties it was as an *aesthete*, a word he brought into popular currency, that he was known; by his tilts, rather spoken than written, against what he considered ugly and drab in furniture and clothes and decoration. His aim was to bring Pre-Raphaelitism into the lives of the English middle-class.

His taste was not very sure, and it cannot be said that the result of his crusade was good. All ideas and speculations take a coarse form when they get down to the run of the people. Thus Nietzsche: his "blond beast" gave women for a time a taste for big, muscular, stupid men with blue eyes and fair hair. That was the practical application. The practical application of Wilde's aesthetic theories was Liberty gowns, and shoddy insecure furniture which became soon far uglier, as it was from the first far less comfortable, than what it replaced. I remember a man in London at the time of Wilde's trial speaking in his favour, and saying with a wave of the hand, "We owe him this!" Now the room we were in was full of horrible bric-à-brac, false antiques, flimsy cane chairs, some kind of vegetation in "aesthetic-blue" pots, and silk window-curtains, pale green. Perhaps Wilde himself would have thought that room hideous; but I am not so sure. Anyhow, he forced stolid British families to put out of doors the beautiful heavy Victorian furniture and curtains, so comfortable, so secure, as we see them in the pictures for Surtees' novels, and to make their houses look like lawn-tennis clubs on the Italian riviera. That seems to me a wonderful feat and such as no other man ever did.

* * *

The development of Wilde's career required, no doubt, special conditions. It required a society tolerant, amusable, and highly intelligent in its upper reaches, and in its lower reaches a docility in following the fashion set. A large number of people with leisure, unharassed lives, "well-off," as the phrase of the time was. All that the later Victorian era afforded. When Remy de Gourmont wrote of Poe that he would have been just as miserable and unlucky in nineteenth-century France as in America, and that what he had need of was an aristocratic society as in England, where the artist is cherished and aided for his own sake and not for the amount of money he earns, he was certainly thinking of that late Victorian Society, perhaps even he was thinking of Oscar Wilde.

If he was, he gave too much importance to the position of Wilde as a writer as a reason for his social success. It may safely be doubted whether many of the aristocratic women of the eighteen-eighties who made much of Wilde and delighted in his company had ever read a line of his. Speaking generally in Gourmont's sense, it cannot be said that English aristocratic society since the reign of Queen Anne to the war had ever shewn special favour to writers; but it had to painters, and, to a certain extent, to musicians.

* * *

Wilde's rise to fame was aided considerably by Du Maurier, the *Punch* artist, and by W. S. Gilbert with *Patience*. Both these satirists give a false impression of Wilde—the impression of a silly tea-cup-and-saucer person, which has in a measure endured to this day; of a man entangled in falsity. So, taking the measure of his stride from that, the French Alexandre Arnoux wrote in

1930: "Wilde was a man who loved so much the *Lie* for its own sake that it is almost impossible, even long after his death, to speak of him according to the truth." Today people are realizing that the "Dr. Railing" of Ibsen's play was not so wrong when he maintained that lies are necessary for human happiness—which is what Wilde maintained independently of Ibsen. How he would be justified at this hour! Science, so exact and inexorable in the nineteenth century, is now tolerable only when mixed with fairy tales. Vast pretence and misrepresentation runs all through the social system. No Government represents itself as it really is; very few families, fewer still individuals.

But Wilde personally gave me the impression of frankness and loyalty to himself and to others, and also of force, and, considering what he was, of singular modesty. Certainly he knew far too well the value of advertisement to resent the caricatures of Du Maurier and Gilbert; and at times he took pleasure in justifying them. Whistler, who missed nothing of all this, and understood Wilde as Swift understood Steele, coming one day on Wilde and Du Maurier talking together, cried out in his disagreeable nasal voice: "Which of you two discovered the other?" It seems that Wilde answered: "We have both discovered you."

The profuse admiration which Wilde displayed for the beautiful Lily Langtry, and for Ellen Terry, the actress, perhaps also helped to draw notice to him. It certainly did to them. At the time of his downfall Mrs. Langtry pretended she had hardly known him. But she lived to see him change from a notorious criminal to an artist famous all over the world, and accordingly she gives the best account we have of Wilde in the years after he left Oxford.

Her account of Wilde in her *Memoirs* is not unfriendly, but it is brutally frank. If he had been in the habit of painting his face, as Carson's biographer will have it, Mrs. Langtry would have said so with the same equanimity as she does say that he did not keep his nails very clean. If other people had not persuaded her that Wilde's admiration was an important ornament of her career and her best chance of being remembered, she would hardly have perceived this herself. Even so, she could not keep out of her account that the devotion of a mere poet, young and little known, counted very small in comparison with the devotion of men high-placed and rich, even when the poet passed a chilly night on her doorstep for the pleasure of catching a glimpse of her as she came home at dawn. There may be women who would be touched by that; she thought it absurd, and one feels sure that at the time she did not like it at all. Taken altogether, there was considerable space between Mrs. Langtry's remembrance of Wilde and his of her. When he spoke of her, which he always did, so far as I can tell, with love and admiration, it was certainly to be inferred that he was of more importance in her life that she allows in her book. She ought to know best.

* * *

Nothing, of course, would have counted if he had not been himself. When I was a boy in New York I knew W. D. Howells and had long talks with him sometimes. One day I spoke of Andrew Lang and Oscar Wilde, lumping them together. Howells stopped me. "It is a different thing. Lang simply lives by literature. Wilde would have invented literature if it had never existed."

I should be ashamed of myself if I did not enter a protest against that. I think Lang, neglected, almost forgotten to-day, was one of the best writers of the English nineteenth century, and more important intellectually than Wilde. As for the literary side, Lang may be said to have shewn Wilde the way to his aesthetic movement. He was a Don at Oxford when Wilde was an undergraduate. One of his early books was called *Ballades in Blue China*—a title which includes the whole thing. Wilde was a greater personality. That is the point I am making. It was his personality, not his literature, that carried him through.

Wilde as a writer had little influence on the youth of the eighteen-nineties, and I have often thought that he did not care for their ideals. He was sympathetically nearer to Ouida, that genius among women, than to the lucid, rather cynical, Max Beerbohm, engaged in reducing human impulses—so far as his characters ever are impulsive—to unsentimental terms. Wilde was not afraid to be sentimental. He remained the Romantic all his life. Not long before his death I heard him praising Charles Reade's *The Cloister and the Hearth*. Somebody who was there—Robert Ross I think—said to him: "You would not like it, Oscar, if you re-read it now." "Ah, perhaps not!" replied Wilde. But he did not seem convinced.

In a notice of Edith Sitwell's *Life of Alexander Pope*, the reviewer cited Wilde's well-known saying: "There are two ways of disliking poetry. One is not to like it, and the other is to read Pope." This judgment, continued the reviewer, like so many other opinions of the nineties, no longer holds sway.

But that was never an opinion of the nineties; it was an opinion of Wilde's, which is something else. Dowson had an intense admiration for Pope, so had Lionel Johnson, so had Beardsley, who illustrated *The Rape of the Lock*. As I have said, a number of the young writers of the eighteen-nineties cared nothing at all for Wilde as an artist. Some were even disrespectful about him till his imprisonment, when they rallied to him because they thought he had been treated unjustly. A lot of minor fry imitated him, of course, but they cannot be taken as typical young writers of the period, and, oddly enough, they were among the most violent against him at the time of his trial. Minor writers for the stage began to lace their dialogues with epigrams after the manner of Wilde, and very afflicting plays most of them turned out. But John Davidson, a good and even great poet ruined by hack-work, and a typical nineties writer, was in all his work the very negative of Wilde. For him Wilde might not have existed. Wilde's sole disciple of any significance among the young writers of that time was a woman, Pearl Craigie, who wrote under the name of

John Oliver Hobbes. All her plays are influenced by Wilde, and her early novels. In her later books, which are her best, the Wilde influence has subsided. Her dilution of Wilde was considered too ladylike in some quarters. Brookfield described her book called *Some Emotions and a Moral* as "A Cup of Tea, *and*—Some Bread and Butter."

Wilde was a character of the Italian Renaissance, or, if you prefer, of Elizabethan England. If he had lived in that time perhaps he would never have written a line. The impulse to write was never with him the primary impulse. The written version was often inferior to the spoken version. And as it happens, his works survive and are admired not as pure works of art, but among those who read him in translations for the philosophy of life they contain.

XI

I HAVE OFTEN THOUGHT THAT he must have suffered in his last years from loneliness—not so much from physical as from moral loneliness. Physical loneliness he could not stand, and to avoid it he seized any measures that offered. So did he take to frequenting a little bar on the boulevard des Italiens with the absurd name "Calisaya"—a place he would never have dreamed of entering in his best days. There he could always find someone to talk to, were it only the bar-tender, and there he did often find a clever and erratic journalist named Ernest La Jeunesse. Wilde's resorting to this place did him harm with the censorious: they accused him of lack of dignity and counted up the number of whiskeys-and-sodas he absorbed daily.

But what was he to do? The censorious took care not to invite him to their houses, took care, in fact, not to shew any interest in him whatever save a malevolent interest. He went to places like "Calisaya" driven by the instinct of self-preservation. He knew that he would go mad if he sat alone with his bitter thoughts. Besides, where was he to sit? In the little room of his hotel with the thousand horrible noises of the cheap hotel? As well be back in his prison cell. Nobody would have come to see him there; he would be as one who had gone down among the dead. Baudelaire has likewise been blamed by old-fashioned biographers for frequenting cafés and dance-halls when he was a man over forty. Baudelaire was impelled by the same reasons as Wilde, but they were nothing like so poignant. Baudelaire was in his own country and among his own people, he had not to endure a punishment which carried with it infamy, nor was he at all so well known as Wilde, and where he was known he was not pointed out with contumely and subjected to the insults of underlings. With Wilde, what must have been the direst form of his suffering was the sense of injustice—a punishment so out of all proportion to his fault.

The Kingdom of Heaven is within us—ay, and the Kingdom of Hell, sometimes.

* * *

But for his moral loneliness there was no remedy bad or good. Except Frank Harris, who did not see him very often or for long spells, there was nobody to whom he could talk of the people and things in his past life which really interested him. Of the other English he saw, some like Leonard Smithers were in a different sphere of life and would not have understood, others were too young—not of his own period. Lord Alfred Douglas, apart from his youth, shared Wilde's views on hardly any subject. Ross too was of another generation: he could hardly be expected to take much interest in the people and happenings of the eighteen-eighties.

Yet as the years passed and the end drew nigh, I noticed in Wilde an ever stronger desire to speak of those first brilliant years when he came to his renown, years which must have been the happiest of his life. Except Harris, who was his contemporary and had known him almost from the beginning, and knew many of the people he knew, he had nobody who could listen with much interest or comprehension when he spoke on this topic; and as he was very careful to adjust his talk to his listeners it was rare that he became reminiscent. Perhaps I was the only one he so favoured, because I was really interested in the heroes of his youth, Ruskin, Carlyle, the Pre-Raphaelites; but I too, with all that, was unsatisfactory, for I could only follow him when he spoke of public figures, and it must have been of other figures known in the London Society of the eighteen-eighties that he wanted to talk. His family, again, he could not often talk about for lack of the right listeners. I was not one; I had met Mrs. Oscar Wilde only once, and his sons I had never set eyes on. He often spoke to me of his mother. I had never seen her either. Of course, there were men and women of his own time in plenty, but they shunned him.

Vincent O'Sullivan

This moral loneliness of his I did not think of at all at the time, but I have since come to realize that it must have been heavy. Practically all the French who considered themselves important, young or old or middle-aged, avoided him. I do not know how well Wilde knew Anatole France, but I should think not very well. They were both famed as talkers, and it is too much to expect of human nature that two famous talkers should be on intimate terms. Anyhow, France, who took no steps that were not calculated, never went near Wilde in his last days and never did anything by word or deed that I ever heard of to aid him. I do not know whether he signed the petition which Stuart Merrill addressed to Lord Rosebery as Prime Minister pleading for Wilde's release from prison; if he refused to do so, he was in numerous company. The vindictiveness and venom with which some of those men replied to Merrill, their insolence towards Wilde, so much a better man than most of them, and that in all ways, moral as well as intellectual, the articles some of them published against him, were a shame to see. The comic touch was supplied by Zola who, like his disciple George Moore, had little sense of humour. Zola, the fat, bearded Zola, father of a well-grown family, indefatigable worker, who never liked to go anywhere without his wife, replied to Merrill that he did not quite understand the document he had received, and that he must refuse to sign it for fear of being compromised in some enterprise against good morals.

But the young men too whom Wilde had known well, Louÿs, Schwob, Henri de Régnier, Stuart Merrill himself, gave the released prisoner the cold shoulder. Even Jean Lorrain and one or two others, notorious for practicing the same vice which put Wilde in prison, left him in the lurch. Lorrain was a journalist, and I heard that his employers told him that if he published a line in defence of Wilde anywhere they would put him off the morning paper from which he derived a good income. The attitude of the others is described in the phrase of one of them: *Je ne fréquente pas les forçats.*

* * *

It must be borne in mind that Wilde was known to by far the greatest part of the French only as a man who had been in an English gaol for a sexual offence. They spoke of him vaguely as a poet, a great writer, but they had nothing to go on. Till the translation of *The Ballad of Reading Gaol* was published, all the French had to go by to form an opinion of Wilde as a writer was *Salome*, which had been given a few times in 1892 at a little "art" theatre in a by-street. Now, when the French talked of the sins and wild life of Verlaine, and added that he was a great poet, they had the printed pages before their eyes. But Wilde they had to take on trust. Wilde's substance as a writer was really known but to a few—Gide, Schwob, Louÿs, Merrill, and three or four others who could read English easily. This I perceived in my talks with the young Jean de Tinan, who was a genius. He thought Wilde was a sort of English Maurice Barrès. That the few who could read his books did so with attention may be inferred from the following passage taken from *Le Livre de Monelle*, by Marcel Schwob:

> All ideas which last are contradiction. All love which lasts is hate. All sincerity which lasts is a lie. All justice which lasts is injustice. All happiness which lasts is sorrow.

There can be no doubt where the inspiration of that comes from.

* * *

The few articles written to defend him by Octave Mirbeau and one or two others used Wilde's case as a pretext to attack the British Government, very unpopular in France at that time. This they did in unbridled terms, not sparing even the private character of the Prime Minister of the day.

On the other hand, the wording of the petition drawn up by Stuart Merrill was cautious and timid. Instead of taking the defendable line that with matters which are in the domain of a man's or woman's conscience—*sins* in the theological sense—the State has nothing to do, the petition described one of the clearest and most well-balanced minds of the time as weak and crazy (*un malheureux fou*). This recalls the wife of a rich baronet, an ex-actress, who wrote to the Home Secretary offering to instal Wilde in the lodge at the gates of her park, where he would be carefully guarded by two strong nurses brought from the nearest asylum. Wilde was greatly amused when this was told him.

The notion that Wilde was mad had gone widely abroad, and at the time of his trial was often heard spoken. Not long after he was sentenced, I was waylaid a few days at Dover by a fierce buffeting tempest which hindered the boats going forth, and in the smoking-room of the Lord Warden Hotel I fell into talk one evening with an army officer garrisoned in the town who had been at Trinity College, Dublin, when Wilde was there. According to this soldier Wilde was certainly mad.

"I'll prove it to you. One night we heard a frightful row in his room. Myself and another man rushed to his door. He was half undressed and jumping about the floor. 'What on earth is the matter?' we asked. 'There's a huge fly in my room,' replied Oscar, 'a great buzzing fly. I can't sleep till I drive it out.' Just think of that! A fly! Nothing I have heard since about him has surprised me. It's ridiculous to put him in prison. What he needs is a nursing-home."

In those days when people talked to you like that it was prudent to agree with them. I am afraid I agreed with the officer.

As an example of the grotesque effect which the Oscar Wilde scandal had upon even intellectual and intelligent Frenchmen may be given a story related by M. Paul Morand. Morand was a schoolboy at the time, and a few years after Wilde was sentenced he was taken by his father on a visit to London. The morning after their arrival his father allowed him to go out alone for a walk in the park. "But," said the father, "if any man with a sunflower in his coat and carrying a lily should speak to you, don't answer him, and run back to the hotel as fast as you can." Morand, a lover of the picturesque, adds with a tinge of regret that he saw no such men in London.

There were certain men, not French, correspondents, some of them, of English or American newspapers, who made it their business to go around Paris talking against Wilde. They used such influence as they had to augment the general hostility. One night, Charles Whibley had Ernest Dowson put out of a café on the Boulevards because Dowson took him to task about his attitude to Wilde. I was not there; but if Dowson had been drinking, as Whibley, who was not in the least a friend of Dowson or of Wilde either, said was the case, then there was some excuse for his action, because Dowson in such a state had an obstinacy and pertinacity which were very aggravating.

Certain English actually accused Wilde of extravagance. "He can't be badly off," they would say, "look what he spends on drink. And he always takes cabs." It was further said that he was always well-dressed.

It is sorrowful to dwell on such disgusting charges. Wilde was not a man to be slovenly if he could avoid it. It is a matter of temperament. By all accounts, Edgar Allan Poe and Baudelaire in their most desperate hours were always neat. As for his drinking, if he had drunk fifty times as much as he did, who would grudge it to him if it relieved even for an hour the pressure of his misery? He was obliged to take cabs because he suffered from a painful malady. This he did not tell me himself: he never, so far as I know, complained of the state of his health. In that and some other matters he had the style of the eighteenth century. "There was no blame attached to anyone for being ill in those days, but people were expected to keep their infirmities to themselves."[6]

---

[6] From the *Life of Gibbon*, by Cotter Morison.

Vincent O'Sullivan

* * *

It is true, as I have said, that he was never in the dire throes of poverty. For one thing, he was not imprisoned in Paris, the cruel city; he was able to change the air from time to time. But he never made the fantastic journeys which have been related in recent years. Not so long ago a Russian traveler reported that he visited a monastery in the Balkans. There he was shewn with great reverence a gold tooth which the monks said had belonged to Oscar Wilde. The story was that Wilde, returning from Constantinople ill and penniless, had sought refuge in the monastery and tarried there some days. When he was leaving, as he had no money to pay his reckoning, he gave the monks his gold tooth.

This is rather a pleasant story. It would perhaps have pleased Wilde himself. And it shews how his fame has spread to remote places. Possibly the monks of the Balkan monastery regard him as a saint. Some time we may hear of miracles wrought there by the relic of Oscar Wilde. After all, *De Profundis* works for edification upon certain temperaments as much as the Confessions of St. Augustine. And what were Augustine's sufferings compared to Wilde's? If terrible sufferings courageously borne, the enduring of dire injustice and reviling without complaint, be matter of saintliness, then Wilde was a saint. What says the prayer of Islam? "O God, make not man endure *all* that he can bear." In Wilde's case this prayer was not heard. It is hard to imagine *moral* suffering, at any rate, which went to a further extreme. For it must be always borne in mind that he had the sense of an injustice committed. Nobody to-day doubts that his punishment was out of proportion to the fault—not only the technical punishment, but its sequel in social persecution.

* * *

He was never at Constantinople in his last years, never in the Balkans. His travels were confined to France and Italy. So far as I know, he never went to Belgium, never stopped off in Switzerland. Once, after he had been ill in Paris, he fared to Rome in the spirit of a pilgrim. That is what he said himself. He went to St. Peter's for a great feast when the Pope was to show himself to the people. "And when I saw the old white Pontiff, successor of the Apostles and Father of Christendom, pass, carried high above the throng, and in passing turn and bless me where I knelt, I felt my sickness of body and soul fall from me like a worn garment, and I was made whole."

He paused and then added: "I wrote to Robbie Ross that I expected to see that my umbrella had blossomed."

This he said, as was his wont, so as not to appear moved. But the emotion was genuine; there were tears, I thought, near his eyes. Tannhäuser! Saint! But no *Elizabeth* to await his return and to ransom his soul by the gift of her own. Instead, at best indifference, loneliness; at worst mockery, insult, the finger of scorn, till the end, and the mean hearse through the streets of Paris.

XII

BY ACCIDENT, I PRESIDED at that first journey of his to Italy a few months after his release, which was not approved of by some of his close friends at the time, and has since been variously commented on.

* * *

Those who have read his biographers know that upon coming out of prison he passed some months at a place on the French coast called Berneval, near Dieppe. One day at the end of that summer, after he had come to Paris, I received a letter from him. He asked if I was in Paris, and if I were would I come to see him.

The next day I went about twelve o'clock to the address given—an hotel in the rue du Helder, just off the Boulevard. He was expecting a friend of his named Rowland Strong. After waiting about a quarter of an hour, seeing that Strong did not turn up, he left a letter for him and we went out to lunch.

In the cab, I asked him who was Rowland Strong? He said he was an English journalist—the Paris correspondent, I think he said, of some London paper, and, what he seemed to think more important, a descendant on his mother's side of Chateaubriand. He seemed in very good spirits and launched out into a description of Strong's valet, an elderly man, who, he said, was the extreme type of the English well-trained servant. When Strong heard that Verlaine was dying, as he did not care to go himself to the mean street and the squalid abode, he sent this man to get news. The valet returned imperturbable.

"Well?" asked Strong.

"I saw the gentleman, sir, and he died immediately."

As Wilde finished this story we arrived at the restaurant, a restaurant chosen by himself, which still exists at the moment of writing, up a flight of stairs over a passage giving on the Boulevard Montmartre, having somehow survived the drastic overhauling of Paris since the war. It was a kind of restaurant where nobody would recognize Wilde, and he did not want to be recognized.

Towards the end of the meal he said that he was rather troubled—as well as I remember, he said he was "passing through a crisis." It seemed that some friends of his family in England wanted him to go into a mountain village and write plays. This, it may be said in passing, was a most stupid suggestion, which took no account of the havoc wrought in his brain and nerves by his trial and imprisonment. What he required was to forget, to be stimulated, distracted from his black thoughts. How could he find that in a mountain village? It would have continued the penal cell. He himself was inclined to go to Italy.

He talked of all this for some time, giving details, some of which it was hard for me to follow from lack of knowledge of the elements of the matter. So far as I remember, the main difficulty was that his wife's friends and relations wanted to keep him from rejoining Lord Alfred Douglas, who was at Naples. Then he added: "I am not telling all this to you because I want advice. I have thought it all out and I would not take advice from anyone." I assured him that nothing was farther from my thoughts than to offer him advice. That indeed was so, both because I should have thought it presumptuous to offer advice to a man so much beyond me both in years and achievement, and also because it was utterly indifferent to me what he did or where he went.

Finally he declared: "I shall go to Italy to-night. Or rather, I would go, but I am in an absurd position. I have no money."

Upon leaving the restaurant we drove to the Banque de Paris et des Pays-Bas in the rue d'Antin where I had an account. He stayed in the cab and I brought him out the sum he wanted. It is one of the few things I look back on with satisfaction. It is not every day that one has the chance of relieving the anxiety of a genius and a hero. I think he left Paris the same evening; certainly very soon. When I saw him next it was a good while after, and in Italy.

* * *

I have sometimes wondered why he did not stay in Italy, by what reasoning he persuaded himself to come back to Paris. Paris killed him. One reason, no doubt, was that it was easier for close friends such as Ross to see him in Paris. But in Italy he would have lived longer, and, I should think, happier. Paris, then, the Dreyfus-case Paris, cannot be figured by the Paris of to-day. To me it seems infinitely preferable. But was it for a man in Wilde's position? In Paris since the war, as in most cities of the west, it is the women's view of life which prevails. All exterior things take their form from that; many interior things too. Now it is well known that women do not take a harsh view of an offence like Wilde's: other kinds of offence seem to them much graver. And for that matter, owing to the feminine influence, it does not seem so grave to Frenchmen of to-day as it did in Wilde's time. It is regarded more as an aberration, perhaps despicable or ludicrous, but not such as should involve disgrace and ruin. In any case, it is certain that a man with the gifts and fame of Oscar Wilde could go where he listed in after-war Paris. Restaurants and theatres would be open to him. He would be extruded from no place where the public in general can go. He would not be pointed out as a monster, nor would children be gathered ostensibly to a stern father's side when he passed in the street. That I saw myself.

Whether such a state of affairs be better or worse, I really do not know. If it be worse, it is the regimen of women which must be blamed who have relaxed the tautness of morals in most directions, if they have tightened them in a few. And thus it has always been, in John Knox's time and all through history, when women got the upper hand.

Wilde endured too much cruelty in the Paris of his time; he received too many wounds, hardly ever resented them openly, but finally died of them. In his book on Wagner, Nietzsche says well that it is a terrible thing for a man who has thought to dominate the world to find he has need of it. And also, it may be added, to find it can hurt him.

XIII

SALOME, A LITTLE PLAY which has had a prodigious fortune, seems, with the recoil of time, among the least good parts of the Wilde production. I have heard it said, and read somewhere, that he wrote it for Sarah Bernhardt. In London, a few years before his trial, I asked him one afternoon if it were true that he was writing a play for Beerbohm Tree. He replied pompously: "I never write plays for anyone. I write plays to amuse myself. After, if people want to act in them, I sometimes allow them to do so." Some months later, the play in question, *A Woman of No Importance*, was produced by Tree at his theatre, and Tree himself played the part of "Lord Illingworth."

But it seems impossible that however infatuated he and those who advised him were with Sarah Bernhardt, however stunned by her tumult, he should ever have thought of her, at the age she had then reached, for the part of "Salome." It is true that when he related to me his projected drama *Isabel*, based on the story of Jezebel in the Bible (2 Kings, ix), he said that he meant it for the French actress; and I understood from him that one or two of his familiars were negotiating with her about it. But Jezebel was a part which Bernhardt could still have played with verisimilitude. "And when Jehu was come to Jezreel, Jezebel heard of it; and she painted her face, and tired her head, and looked out at a window." Sarah Bernhardt could still represent a mature woman of that kind.

But Salome was a child. Even following the Gospel narrative without criticism, she was little more than a child. It is a hard strain on plausibility to see Wilde's "Salome" played by even a young actress—young as actresses are when they are thought capable of tackling such a part, which is not in the first blush of youth by any means. I have seen a few.

The best performance I recall was by a Russian, Ysovskaya, in Berlin some years after the war. But to appreciate her show you had to make all sorts of concessions on general grounds. Also on the particular ground of Wilde's text. Her "Salome" was a woman scourged by her passions. Rather a noble character, a victim of fate. Evidently the idea underlying this reading of the part was that Salome never believed the prophet could be killed; she believed that a miracle would strike the sword from the headsman's clutch. In the last scene of all it was not insane sensuality that was suggested, but the collapse of a woman who sees that a god can die.

That this reading is far from Wilde's conception, all who have his text in mind will agree. Still, that the chief part can be ennobled in such a fashion, that it will bear various interpretations, shows that the play is not merely the artificial morbid thing it has often been described. For all that, it seems preferable to see "Salome" in the opera of Richard Strauss. The music is precisely the right music. It carries the drama through with such a rush that it is impossible to linger on the details.

Some of these, when thought over calmly, must give us pause. Wilde took his story, as he had every right to do, just as he found it in St. Mark's Gospel. Certain difficulties in the story he made no account of. It apparently did not occur to him that, seeing the immemorial custom of oriental courts, it was to the last degree unlikely that a princess should dance and make an exhibition of herself at a banquet for soldiers and courtiers. This consideration, which would have weighed heavily with Flaubert, who inspired to a considerable extent the scenery and the language of the play, Wilde neglected, as he was justified in doing by the Gospel narrative. But neither in the Gospel narrative nor in Josephus could he have found any authority for making his Herod a wreck of a man trembling at the shadows of the moon.

Wilde's play goes aside of the drama in the Gospel story. It is curious that he did not perceive that the real heroine about whose figure the drama should move is not the child but the mother. But to get an actress capable of playing "Salome," you must search

Vincent O'Sullivan

among women with considerable experience. This carries the obligation of representing Herodias as a woman about fifty. But, historically speaking, she must have been still a young woman.

* * *

In *Salome*, in all his plays, and in all he wrote, Wilde had something that no one else had had before or since. In the various pieces which have been put before the world since his death and ascribed to him—one of them the effort of a spiritualistic medium—it is easy for anyone familiar with the genuine work to detect the lack of his peculiar magic. It was in great part this magic which carried his plays to a public composed of various elements. Mrs. Craigie used the same furniture as Wilde: witticisms, epigrams, fine people; her plays were produced at the same theatre as Wilde's before the same public; but they had not the same vitality and nothing like the same popularity. Yet they were good plays of their kind, and for a fastidious taste not so jarring as Wilde's are in many parts of them. But it was just the coarse strain in Wilde which made the popularity of his plays. He was sentimental in his dramas—not at all aristocratic. Now the populace in all countries are sentimental. Since the last war, the popular taste being the only taste that counts, there is a deluge of sentiment all over—lushy films, end-in-a-kiss dramas, and incredibly silly ditties which seem the last babblings before total idiocy and extinction:

> You're my m-o-o-n,
> I'm your honey-c-o-o-mb.

But the Wilde plays have more than the coarse sentiment which was the immediate cause of their success. A work of art conveys a message which is valueless to the recipient unless it be understood by the sender, and the message he undertook to send to the public was perfectly clear to Wilde. Unlike English dramatists who were working at the same time, Pinero, Henry Arthur Jones, and some others, the accidents of the plot did not interest him so much as the sentiments and emotions of the characters. The skill, the facility, were generally controlled. It is evident to the onlooker that he wants to produce authentic work and to construct loyally without having recourse to theatricalism. That he usually succeeds in doing this is proved by the shock experienced when he does fall down to the old Scribe and Sardou tricks—Lady Windermere's fan, Lord Illingworth's glove.

His best personages are conducted through the drama with such vigour and logic that it becomes impossible for them to escape their particular truth. This is especially true of *A Woman of No Importance*. When his farce, *The Importance of Being Earnest*, was revived in London some twenty-five years after it was written, the women wore Beardsley costumes. That kind of thing is a mistake in the case of Wilde. What his plays need is to be played frankly and largely in the spirit of the hour in which they are being played. They are not at all historical or periodicals. The sentiments and situations are popular and sentimental, and therefore of constant appeal. The terms "demi-monde," "light woman," may have disappeared, but there are always, and even more now than in Wilde's time, Mrs. Erlynnes'. People in general are more tolerant now towards the rich woman with an invisible husband, towards the charming girl who has a mother who is gossiped about; but, as a matter of fact, many people were equally tolerant at the time Wilde produced his plays. His plays cannot be taken as pictures of the eighteen-nineties, for the very good reason that they are pictures of a society which Wilde saw in permanence through the eyes of Scribe and Dumas the Younger. The chief difference, and perhaps the only difference between Wilde's characters and such characters as they are presented to-day, is that all his more or less tarnished people yearn for respectability. To-day they would yearn for money, balm of all bruises.

His plays are moral. There is not as with Dumas, Augier, and certain English dramatists of Wilde's time, a rather pedantic friend of the family who emits general moral reflections suggested by the case in hand. The moral comes out of the scenes, and it is very obviously there. It may seem strange to think of Wilde as having in mind a moral lesson, but on re-reading his plays one is struck by the facility with which he runs into moralizing—indirect moralizing, it is true, cut by flippant remarks of a scepticism entirely superficial. The end of his dramas is always a moral lesson. Baudelaire, long ago, referring to Augier and his school, declared that the wages of sin is *not* death, but in many cases success and riches. But that is not at all the spirit of the Wilde dramas. In them the virtuous win out in the end, and as for the wicked, it would not be pleasant to be in their shoes.

The French writer I have already quoted, Alexandre Arnoux, speaking of *De Profundis*, says that from the silence of the prison rose an extraordinary lyrical cry of such humanity, simplicity, and depth of thought as no one ever expected to hear from the brilliant, paradoxical, and often superficial aesthete. If *Salome* be entirely artificial, and *The Importance of Being Earnest* a comedy which does not go deep into motives, in Wilde's three dramas, all the qualities which the critic praises in *De Profundis* are latent, and even at times active. Underneath the armour of mockery and worldliness in which he affronted his time, Wilde was serious and reverent. He was never cynical as Thackeray is. *Salome* apart, there is no more vice in his plays—or for the matter of that in all his work—than in the plays of Victor Hugo. Situations which Racine dared Wilde would never have dared. He was a Romantic with a sense of humour. He took the form of drama he found already made. He did not create a new form more than Shakespeare.

XIV

He [Wilde] must have had a fund of information about many interesting people of the nineteenth century, things told him, and things he had observed himself. I did not profit by all that at the time, and now I am sorry. But it was not easy, at least not for me, to bring him into a desired track. He had sometimes the American orator's trick of raising his voice peremptorily to beat down an interruption he foresees.

I here set down some traits which seem worth preserving.

* * *

Of Rossetti he said:

"Rossetti was much blamed for his morbid conduct after his wife's death. As you know, he put the manuscript of a book of poems he was going to publish into his wife's coffin, and years after the coffin had to be dug up and the poems were recovered by Watts. Rossetti cloistered himself, lived only by night, and took sleepy drugs. People said such grief was excessive.

"But Rossetti had more on his mind than his wife's death. He felt he had killed her. One night, Rossetti with his wife and Swinburne went to dine at a restaurant. Before dinner she had taken a dose of chloral. At dinner she drank some wine, and began to act so stupidly that the other diners in the place were scandalized. Rossetti became very angry. When they got back home she said she wanted some more chloral. He took the phial and thrust it roughly into her hands saying: 'There! take the lot!' Then he and Swinburne went off together. When he returned in the dawn his wife was unconscious with the phial empty beside her."[7]

---

[7] In reading a translation of Miss Violet Hunt's book, *The Wife of Rossetti*, which appeared in *La Revue Hebdomadaire* during 1935, I found that the account there given of Mrs. Rossetti's end is substantially the same as that of Wilde as reported in the text.

Vincent O'Sullivan

* * *

"One day William Morris was telling Rossetti the scheme of a poem which he meant to write. It was a poem of the Middle-Ages, about a knight who had a dragon for a brother. Rossetti, who was in a bad humour, kept repeating contemptuously: 'A dragon for a brother! A dragon for a brother!'

"Morris lost patience. 'Well, Gabriel,' he said briskly, 'it is better to have a dragon for a brother than a fool for a brother.'

"Rossetti was taken aback. 'Ah, yes,' he said thoughtfully after a pause. 'There's not much to be said for William Michael.'"[8]

In all Wilde said about Rossetti he confirmed Hall Caine's account of the poet. Rossetti did not much like Morris, and one of Morris's characteristics he despised. Rossetti, who was the soul of generosity himself, thought that the penuriousness of Morris, who was rich, corresponded ill with his fine humanitarian sentiments. "Did anyone ever hear of Topsy giving a penny to anybody?" Rossetti would ask.

* * *

"Swinburne, like Dickens and others, was a great admirer of the circus-rider, Adah Isaacs Menken, who eventually married the prize-fighter Heenan, probably the only man (said Wilde) she ever really cared about. Swinburne she used to call her little red-haired poet. One night they were dining together in a private room in a restaurant, and Swinburne suddenly threw himself on Menken and bit her bare arm. Thereupon Menken, who had the muscular arm of a tamer of horses, felled him to the ground. Then she rang and called the waiters, and worked over Swinburne herself, and they brought him round.

"'Darling,' said Swinburne, 'why did you fell me to the ground?'

---

[8] W. M. Rossetti, editor of the poems of his brother, and of his sister Christina.

"'Ah,' she replied, 'why did you bite me?'

"'I did that,' said Swinburne, 'because I love you.'"

Swinburne, as it is well known, after a rather troubled youth, retired to Theodore Watts-Dunton's house at Putney, where he lived for the rest of his life. This fact roused in Wilde the most extraordinary resentment whenever he thought of it. "You know, Watts is a solicitor and the business of a solicitor is to conceal crime. Swinburne's genius has been killed, and Watts is doing his best to conceal it."[9]

* * *

Wilde's opinion of this case was wrong. Like most other people he was unjust to Watts, who was a kind man and a good critic and poet. He had nothing whatever to gain by having Swinburne in his house. In fact, he refused when the arrangement was proposed to him. But Lady Jane Swinburne, Swinburne's mother, felt that her son would die if left to himself, and it was to her prayers that Watts yielded. Swinburne himself refused to live with anybody but Watts—that is, I suppose, of those willing to take him in. Watts only took him on condition that if he proved rowdy or scandalous he would have to go.

But the idea of any kind of narrow life annoyed Wilde. Tennyson's life also he disapproved of. "How can a man be a great poet and lead the life of an English country-gentleman? Think of a man going down to breakfast at eight o'clock with the family and writing *Idylls of the King* till lunchtime!" However, he admired Tennyson. He once cited as a perfect line of poetry:

> Now lies the earth all Danae to the stars.

---

[9] Readers of *The Gentle Art of Making Enemies* will remember that Whistler viewed with the same contempt Swinburne's retirement to Putney. "I have lost a friend; I have gained an acquaintance: Algernon Swinburne Esq., Putney."

Once, when he was talking thus contemptuously of Tennyson's mode of life, somebody objected that a far greater genius, Victor Hugo, also led a bourgeois life. Wilde would not have this at all. "Hugo was mingled in all the great events of his time and country. During all the Empire he was an exile."

* * *

When Longfellow came to England he was invited to Windsor. The Queen said some kind things to him, whereupon Longfellow answered that he was pleased and surprised to find he was so well known in England. Then said the Queen: "Oh, I assure you, Mr. Longfellow, you are very well known. All my servants read you."

During Wilde's visit to the United States Longfellow told this to him laughing, and added that sometimes when he was lying awake at night he used to wonder whether it were a mere oversight or was deliberately intended. Wilde said it was the rebuke of Majesty to the vanity of the poet.

He had an immense admiration for Victoria and liked to talk about her. Caton Woodville, who was commissioned to paint the official picture of the Queen at the service in Westminster Abbey during the Jubilee of 1887, told Wilde that he was debating whether he should give the Queen her natural high colour. Wilde advised him to give her the pallor of Majesty. But when the Queen saw the picture her first remark was that her face did not look natural. According to Wilde her words were: "Mr. Woodville, we are redder than that."

When Bastien Lepage, who was certainly not an academic painter, was in England, he received an invitation to a royal garden-party. When he saw the Queen passing across the lawn, he was so fascinated by her charm and regal demeanour, that he said to Wilde: "I would give anything to paint her. You must get me permission. It will be the picture of my life." Wilde accordingly mentioned the matter to the Prince of Wales, who promised to do what he could, but added that he had not much hope of success. And, in fact, Bastien Lepage never painted the Queen, who kept to her official painters.

* * *

When Ravachol, the Anarchist, was killed in Paris, Wilde went with some friends to view the body. One of the things which struck him was that the young man's fingers were brown up to the knuckles from cigarette smoking. Wilde lifted the head and was astonished at the weight of it. Then he recalled the end of Flaubert's story with the words about John the Baptist which run somehow thus: "The three carried the head by turns, for it was very heavy." "Flaubert's father was a doctor," said Wilde.

* * *

"Great antipathy shews secret affinity," he said.
"Then you have an affinity to George Moore?"
"No; but perhaps to Zola. Still, I hope not."

* * *

He published his poem *The Sphinx* in a very limited edition. To one who remarked this to him, he answered: "My first idea was to print only three copies: one for myself, one for the British Museum, and one for Heaven. I had some doubt about the British Museum."

* * *

When I was publishing a book of poems, I told him that Beardsley was designing the cover. He urged me to oblige Leonard Smithers to print Beardsley's design on both sides of the cover: "Nothing looks more vulgar and cheap than a book with an ornament on one side of the cover and the other side blank."

* * *

He had a great admiration for Arthur James Balfour. One day when he was praising him a friend of his, a journalist, remarked: "Balfour is only his uncle's nephew."

"Really?" said Wilde, much vexed. "And how many uncles have nephews like Arthur Balfour?"

* * *

The Savile Club in London, made up of writers, doctors, scientists, etc., shewed great animosity to Wilde. Perhaps he was even blackballed there. One day when he was lunching in the club with a member, he said: "I feel like a lion in a den of Daniels."

* * *

He told me that a friend of his was quite content to die when the doctors told him he had a malady unknown in the annals of medicine. He thought that to die of the ordinary ills which afflict humanity would be too humiliating.

* * *

His father and his brother had the same name. One day a girl wrote a letter to young Wilde to say that he was responsible for her unborn child. The father opened the letter by mistake, and when Willie Wilde came down to breakfast the elder man said indignantly: "Here is a most disgraceful letter." Willie read the letter, and then looked up and said blandly: "Well, sir, what are you going to do about it?"

* * *

When Wilde was first imprisoned in Holloway after the libel action, one of his friends asked him what book he would like. Wilde replied: "Flaubert's *Salammbô*." The friend, who was religious, cried out: "It is that sort of nonsense which has brought you where you are." Whereupon Wilde said that he would like *The Confessions of Saint Augustine*. But, so far as I know, this is a book which never made much impression on him.

* * *

It was while reading the Bible in prison, at a time, as he explained, when no other book was allowed, that the ideas came to him for his two plays. He read the account of Jezebel and Jehu and said to himself: "There is something wrong here—things left out. That is not the full account of the matter." He made some connexion between Jezebel and Isabel which I did not grasp. I remember thinking at the time that from a philological point of view it was impossible; but I took care not to say this to Wilde, who no doubt perceived himself that his notion was fantastic. His aim was to bring out that Queen Jezebel was not the "bedizened hussy," termagant and shrew, which her name connoted in the popular estimation.

The other play was to deal with the captivity of Israel in Egypt, and the legend of Joseph.

* * *

He said the penalty for talking in prison was very severe. Old prisoners learned to talk without moving their lips. One day as the prisoners were exercising in a row in the yard, he heard a voice behind him: "What are you doing here, Dorian Gray?"

To remain silent before such a question was impossible for Wilde even if he were to be shot the next minute: "Not Dorian Gray, Lord Henry Wotton."

A few days later he heard the same voice: "I have been at every one of your first nights and at every day of your three trials."

"As if," said Wilde, telling the story rather moved, "they were the great events of the poor fellow's life."

* * *

I gave him Baudelaire's letters, but he did not like them: "They are all about publishers and money. His real self was in his poetry."

It is easy to understand that he did not want to read anything painful or unpleasant after he came out of gaol.

* * *

He professed an admiration for Disraeli, but to me at least he never talked much about him. He seemed to think it a poor end for so much ambition to end as leader of a political party in Parliament. Parnell he put higher because he led a people. "It was really extraordinary the power which Parnell had in Ireland, and his control over his party in the House. One night, when the Irish had won an important division amid the wildest excitement, one of the Irish members (Healy) turned to Parnell and shouted: "Sure, it's a great night for Ireland, Parnell!" "Mr. Parnell, I suppose you mean," replied the calm Parnell freezingly.

About Parnell he repeated one of his favourite sayings: "There is something vulgar in all success. The greatest men fail—or seem to the world to have failed."

* * *

"The greatest artists are stupid and tiresome men as a rule. Flaubert was certainly a stupid man. But bad poets and novelists are romantic and delightful."

* * *

"What are you doing? It is all equal whether one does something or not. Create yourself. Be yourself your poem."

* * *

He said of the statue of Gambetta near the Louvre in Paris, that Gambetta looked as if he were trying to escape from a *bordel* without paying and two women were pulling him back by the tails of his coat.

* * *

When *The Ballad of Reading Gaol* was published, Leonard Smithers, the publisher, received this letter from an undergraduate at Cambridge: "Sir, were it superfluous to suggest that he did not wear a scarlet coat because he was in the Blues?"[10]

* * *

Wilde told me that when Maupassant visited London he was the guest of Henry James. James took him to the Exhibition at Earl's Court and they dined in the restaurant. Maupassant said: "There's a woman sitting over there that I'd like to have. Go over and get her for me."

James was horribly shocked.

"But, my dear friend, I can't do that. She may be perfectly respectable. In England you have to be careful."

After a few minutes, Maupassant spotted another woman.

"Surely, you know her at least? I could do quite well with her if you'll get her for me. Ah, if I only knew English!"

---

10 It should perhaps be pointed out for the benefit of American readers that this is a double pun: there are two regiments of Life Guards—Blue and Red.

When James had refused for about the fifth time, Maupassant observed sulkily: "Really you don't seem to know anybody in London."

That James had refused to do what he asked from motives of prudery and respectability never occurred to him.

Epilogue

This book grew out of an article which, when finished, was found to be too long for a magazine. In making it into a book, the original article was not discarded but built around, a piece here and one there, as time and inclination permitted. Hence it is not combed and brushed with the neat precision of a treatise which accumulates from the first sentence following a foreseen plan.

This has one advantage. A preconceived biography requires for its orderly and complete development a regular termination in which all the material is relied on to furnish out a final chapter pitched in the tone of a judgment to accuse or attenuate by means of accidents taken in a life from childhood onward.

Nothing of the kind can be needed or expected here. Still, enough has been told of Wilde in the foregoing pages to enable the reader to come to some conclusion as to the kind of man he was. The historic Wilde can only be discovered at the extremity of a number of legendary Wildes. All writing of this kind implies an arbitrary element, each writer, however objective, being unable to avoid putting something of himself into the picture. Here, at least, the *nature* of the report is not mythic, or drawn from the writings of others which are subject to indefinite corrections. Such as the portrait is, it is drawn from the life. But we can be sure that something imaginary arises from the contemplation of the real which is far more nutritious than the real itself.

Oscar Wilde will doubtless survive because he had a doctrine which is based on some elemental facts of human nature; whereas a man like George Moore, for instance, who had only temporary opinions about art, is already never quoted and must soon be totally forgotten. The generosity of Wilde made him the vulgarizer of Rossetti, Pater, Ruskin: he gave to these a glow of brave daily life which they lacked. It is the vulgarizer always who is slaughtered. But Wilde has not been slaughtered, nor will be for a good while to come, we may now be sure.

And this because he was a vast deal more than the vulgarizer of Ruskin, Pater, Rossetti, and also of William Morris. He was in some ways superior to any of them—superior a good deal to Morris and Pater, and superior even to Ruskin. Say again, *in some ways*; not by any means in all. By the word "vulgarizer," used often in this book, it is not meant that he let them down any. On the contrary. If he did not elevate them, he broadened their scope of appeal. Were the word "popularizer" a word not so ugly to see and to hear, that were the word to carry what is meant.

Morris worked out to Morris furniture, and Liberty gowns, and studies in green, and green silk curtains; Pater, taken with Rossetti, to sunflowers, to lilies, to feeling faint at sunsets and at the sight of stately persons; Ruskin to a philosophy of art which would portray nothing that is sad and relate nothing that is ugly.

Upon all this came clanging down prison bars, consternation, silence. And then, as from a single instrument in what was once a vast orchestra, some sad imploring notes for pity, for pardon, not so much for himself as for the stumbling and fallen everywhere. A note soon hushed, but with echoes which will live long yet in the hearts of the oppressed, the accused, and those whose heads are bent down upon their riveted hands.

There is no doubt that the art of Wilde has gone out of fashion. There is no doubt that many young men and women feel themselves as remote from Wilde as from (say!) Matthew Arnold. But also, this can only be applied to certain parts of his work. On the other hand, there is hardly an author more quoted in all Europe. Where he has thought, he survives.

The opinion of older generations on this matter does not offer much interest, being churned up with all sorts of prejudices of their time which seem to have survived even to this day in some quarters.

Wilde often mixed his colours in his purely decorative work, and that is the part of his work which is weather-stained and peeling off. One of the reasons is that with all his self-assurance he was self-distrustful, and followed too humbly his masters. One of these, perhaps the chief, was Flaubert—certainly Flaubert and Pater. Now from Flaubert there is to-day a general stampede. Possibly from Pater too, but that is not so easy to observe, for Pater never had the wide fame and influence of Flaubert.

In following Flaubert Wilde was going against his nature. No two men have been essentially more different, no two artists farther apart. The long slow labour in the summer-time and sad winters; the same fragment taken from the anvil fifty times and then replaced to be hammered into a fairer shape—how impossible was all that for Wilde! Flaubert said he had slept with the French grammar, meaning thereby that he knew it as a man knows his wife. But it may be doubted if that is the best way to know it, if it be not a mistake to know it too well in its intimate details with the sponge in its hand and the soapsuds on arms and breast. In Flaubert, in Pater too, there are any number of good things which are swamped, almost obliterated, by the panoply of style. You begin to feel that both are thinking more about how they tell what happened than of what happened. And that is certainly what was called in the seventeenth century euphuism or preciosity, and what was practised long before the seventeenth century by many writers, and most flagrantly by Saint Augustine. But Wilde cannot be accused of that, or rather no more than Dickens, who wrote often enough, Heaven knows! when the inspiration had given out, a tinsel garish rhetoric which nobody can bear any longer.

It is surely open to question whether anybody of his time—say, between 1880 and 1900—wrote better than Oscar Wilde when he is at his best. And there are pages and pages where he is at his best. The traces of Flaubert and Pater float on the surface; really, he is quite individual. This has been acknowledged by some of those least in sympathy with the man and his attitude to life. Among his characteristics, he has a gift of creating by dense phrases an atmosphere so heavy that it has all the weight of tragedy. Many others of his time and since have tried to do that, and generally the result of the effort has been miasmal, sodden, with the newspaper growl-boys and sob-sisters well placed. Altogether, Wilde is not a master to be recommended to those who are trying to write good English. But all the same, he is a master, I think.

He had the artistic temperament to an unlimited extent. The poetic temperament too he had, and was at times a true poet, but never a great poet. He missed being that, not because he had no heart, as they have sometimes said, but because he had no interior life. By this is meant that condition in which men and women have colloquies with their soul and take knowledge of it; are impelled to prayer and to contact with the prime forces of our being; come to secret terms with their passions either to satisfy or to suppress them. It is a condition usually ascribed to some form of religion, and Teresa of Ávila, the Spanish nun of the sixteenth century, is as good an example as any of the interior life developed by religion. But Nietzsche must have had as intense an inner drama as Saint Teresa. Wilde was totally devoid of an interior life. He was a man of the city, and of the heart of the city—the market-place. He liked what Gautier said about himself: "I am a man for whom the visible world exists." For Wilde the visible world is life in society. You will search in vain through his books for any genuine reaction to the prime contacts of our being—the sea, the great winds, rain, and the night. His has been called "a great romantic intellect"; but in this indifference to all life that is not social human life he is in the classical tradition of the eighteenth century. He shuns the mysterious; and in himself he was not mysterious, nor had he the aura of mystery and its attractions. It is not in the desert that his Sphinx proposes her riddles, but in a room—a room in an hotel.

Biographical notes

Amiel, Henri Frederic (1821–81) Swiss writer, moral philosopher and professor of aesthetics. Known for his *Journal Intime* which contained his meditations and thoughts on religion.

Anne, Queen (1665–1714) monarch of England, Scotland, Wales and Ireland from 1702 to 1707 and then, following the 1707 Act of Union, as queen of Great Britain and Ireland.

Apollinaire, Guillaume (1880–1918) a French novelist, playwright and poet. He coined the term "surrealism". Arrested and detained by Parisian police for a week in 1911 on suspicion of stealing the *Mona Lisa* and other items from the Louvre museum. He was released without charge.

Apuleius (Lucius Apuleius Madaurensis c.124–c.170) a writer and philosopher of the Roman Empire. *Florida* is a collection of his speeches delivered in Africa.

Archer, William (1856–1924) a Scottish writer and critic. He was an early promoter and translator into English of Henrik Ibsen's (q.v.) work.

Arnold, Matthew (1822–88) an English poet and critic.

Arnoux, Alexandre (1884–1973) a French screenwriter.

Augier, Guillaume Victor Émile (1820–89) a French dramatist.

Balfour, Arthur (1848–1930) a British statesman who was prime minister from 1902 to 1905. His uncle was Lord Salisbury (Robert Gascoyne-Cecil) an earlier prime minister whom Balfour once served under. Some people attribute the phrase "Bob's your uncle" to this nepotism.

Balzac, Honoré de (1799–1850) a French writer and critic. The series of novels that compose *La Comédie humaine* are seen as his most significant work.

Barbey d'Aurevilly, Jules-Amédée (1808–89) a French novelist favoured by the *fin-de-siècle* decadents.

Barrès, Maurice (1862–1923) a French novelist, journalist and politician. One of his works was *Le Culte du moi*, a trilogy of novels.

Bastien Lepage, Jules (1848–84) a French artist associated with the beginning of naturalism.

Baudelaire, Charles (1821–67) a French poet and translator. Some of his work resulted in him being fined by the French authorities for offending public morals.

Beardsley, Aubrey (1872–98) an English artist and author. He produced line drawings in black ink (which suited the printing technology of the time) in an often erotic and grotesque style.

Beddoes, Thomas Lovell (1803–49) an English poet and physician. His work showed his obsession with death. He died by poisoning himself.

Beerbohm Tree, Sir Herbert (1852–1917) an English actor and manager of the Haymarket Theatre in London.

Beerbohm, Sir Henry Maximilian (1872–1956) an English essayist and caricaturist. He knew Wilde from Oxford University and by way of his half-brother Herbert Beerbohm Tree (q.v.).

Belgiojoso, Princess (Cristina Trivulzio di Belgiojoso, 1808–71) an Italian writer and journalist. Her activities in promoting Italian independence caused her to seek safety in Paris.

Bennett, Arnold (1867–1931) a prolific English novelist. He was looked down on by some writers during his

Biographical notes

lifetime: Virginia Woolf described him as having "a shopkeeper's view of literature".

Bernard Shaw, George (1856-1950) an Irish playwright. He was the author or many plays and received the Nobel Prize for literature in 1925.

Bernhardt, Sarah (1844-1923) a French actress. Wilde wrote *Salomé* with her in mind, although she never performed in the role as the play was censored in Britain.

Bonaparte, Marie Princess (Princess George of Greece, 1882-1962) a French author and psychoanalyst. The book referred to in footnote 4 is *The Life and Works of Edgar Allan Poe: A Psycho-Analytic Interpretation* (with a foreword by Sigmund Freud) it was translated into English and published in 1949.

Bosie *see* Douglas, Lord Alfred.

Brookfield, Charles (1857-1913) a British actor and playwright. The text says that his mother was a lady-in-waiting to Queen Victoria (q.v.) although this appears to be unverifiable; his father was honorary chaplain to Queen Victoria. His mother was a friend of William Makepeace Thackeray (q.v.) with whom she enjoyed a platonic relationship. Brookfield was the first actor to portray Sherlock Holmes on stage.

Browning, Robert (1812-89) an English poet and author. In Wilde's 1890 essay "The Critic as Artist", he describes Browning: "He is the most Shakespearean creature since Shakespeare. If Shakespeare could sing with myriad lips, Browning could stammer through a thousand mouths. ... Yes, Browning was great. And as what will he be remembered? As a poet? Ah, not as a poet! He will be remembered as a writer of fiction, as the most supreme writer of fiction, it may be, that we have ever had."

Buloz, François (1803-77) a French editor. He edited *Revue des deux Mondes* which published some of the leading French authors of the time.

Bulwer-Lytton, Edward (1803-73) an English writer. He is not such a popular author today although he is remembered through the annual Bulwer-Lytton Fiction Contest, which awards a prize for "an atrocious opening sentence to a hypothetical bad novel". This is in response to one of Bulwer-Lytton's own efforts: "It was a dark and stormy night."

Burke, Edmund (1729-97) an Irish philosopher and politician. Considered by some as an early Conservative.

Byron, Lord George Gordon (1788-1824) an English poet who was a major figure in Romanticism.

Carlyle, Thomas (1795-1881) a Scottish historian and author. He contended that "the history of the world is but the biography of great men". His *The French Revolution: A History*, published in 1837 is considered a contentious work because of his writing style.

Carson, Edward (1854-1935) an Irish politician and barrister. The Marquess of Queensbury (q.v.) hired Carson to defend him in the 1895 libel case against Wilde. Carson had known Wilde as a child and as a student at Trinity College in Dublin. Wilde was supposed to have said, "No doubt he will pursue his case with all the added bitterness of an old friend."

Castlereagh, Lady (Amelia Anne "Emily" Stewart, Marchioness of Londonderry, 1772-1829) was the wife of the British foreign secretary during the Napoleonic Wars (1803-

15) and an influential member of London "society".

Caton Woodville, Richard Jr. (1856–1927) an English artist. He was particularly known for illustrating battle scenes. The painting of Queen Victoria (q.v.) during her Jubilee (60 years reigning in 1897) mentioned in the text was perhaps "For Queen and Empire: Queen Victoria reviewing the Imperial Contingents at Windsor, Diamond Jubilee, 1897".

Champfleury (Jules François Felix Fleury-Husson, 1821–89) a French art critic and novelist.

Chateaubriand, François-René de (1768–1848) a French politician. During the French Revolutionary Wars (1792–1802) he was wounded and exiled in England for a while.

Chekhov *see* Tchekov.

Choderlos de Laclos, Pierre Ambroise François (1741–1803) a French novelist and army general. He is best remembered for *Les Liaisons dangereuses* (1782).

Cholmondeley, Mary (1859–1925) an English novelist. Her best-selling book was *Red Pottage* published in 1899. It does not include the line mentioned in the text but has similar ones: "Each little twig and twiglet was made manifest, raw gold against the twilight that lurked beneath the heavy boughs" and "There was a momentary silence, like that which travellers tell us succeeds the roar of the lion in his primeval forest, silencing even the twitter of the birds."

Chopin, Fryderyk Franciszek (1810–49) a Polish composer. During his relationship with Amantine Dupin (better known as George Sand, q.v.) he stayed at her house in Nohant in France. He wrote several of his famous piano works at the house.

Christ, Jesus (c.4BC–AD30) the central figure on Christianity. Prior to his arrest and trial by the Sanhedrin, the Agony in the Garden of Gethsemane describes Jesus praying, "O my Father, if this cup may not pass away from me, except I drink it, thy will be done." The cup (or chalice in the text) is metaphor for the suffering and pain he is about to take suffer.

Clarke, Sir Edward (1841–1931) a British barrister and politician. He represented Wilde in his case of libel against the Marquess of Queensbury (q.v.). Subsequently he also attempted to defend Wilde against 25 charges of "gross indecencies and conspiracy to commit gross indecencies". During the trial Wilde was asked "What is 'the Love that dare not speak its name'?"

Clifford Barney, Natalie (1876–1972) an American writer who hosted a literary salon in her home in Paris. She had met Wilde when she was a child and later had relationships with Dolly Wilde (q.v.) and Olive Custance (q.v.).

Coburg (Prince Frederick Josias of Saxe-Coburg-Saalfeld, 1737–1815) was an Austrian general during the Napoleonic Wars (1803–15).

Coleridge, Samuel Taylor (1772–1834) an English poet. A founder of the English Romantic movement and well known for his poems such as *The Rime of the Ancient Mariner* and *Kubla Khan*. De Quincey (q.v.) wrote a series of essays, including one on Coleridge, collected together as *Recollections of the Lake Poets* (1834–40). Here, De Quincy, despite knowing Coleridge for several years, wrote a forthright description of his subject that led one reviewer to describe De Quincy as "a calumniator, cowardly spy, traitor, base betrayer of the hos-

Biographical notes

pitable social hearth," and "one of the greatest scoundrels living!"

Conder, Charles (1868–1909) an English painter. He returned to Europe after living in Australia for several years. In 1895, he went to Dieppe in France and mixed with the artistic community there. He was described as "a sick man, unable to face reality". It is said that in Dieppe he met Aubrey Beardsley (q.v.) and that they disliked each other.

Congreve, William (1670–1729) a playwright and poet. He was born in England but was taken to Ireland with his parents when a baby. Educated in Ireland, he returned to England where he wrote Restoration-era plays.

Corelli, Marie (Mary Mackay, 1855–1924) an extremely successful English novelist. Inevitably, her work attracted criticism from some: "a woman of deplorable talent who imagined that she was a genius, and was accepted as a genius by a public to whose commonplace sentimentalities and prejudices she gave a glamorous setting" and as having "the imagination of a Poe with the style of an Ouida and the mentality of a nursemaid".

Cotter Morison, James Augustus (1832–88) an English historian. His book on Edward Gibbon (1737–94) was published in 1878 (*English Men of Letters: Gibbon*). Gibbon was an English historian famous for *The History of the Decline and Fall of the Roman Empire* (1776–88).

Crackanthorpe, Hubert (1870–96) an English writer who published a few novels and many short stories in magazines such as *The Yellow Book*.

Craigie, Pearl (1867–1906) a writer who used the name John Oliver Hobbes. She had been born in the USA and moved with her parents to London as a baby. Her first book, *Some Emotions and a Moral*, published in 1891, was a massive success. She had been brought up as a Nonconformist but converted to Catholicism in 1892.

Custance, Olive Eleanor (1874–1944) an English poet who was part of the Decadent movement. While in a relationship with Natalie Clifford Barney (q.v.) she became attached to Lord Alfred Douglas (q.v.) and the couple eventually married in 1902.

d'Agoult, Mme. (Marie Catherine Sophie, Comtesse d'Agoult, 1805–76) a Franco-German author. After leaving her husband, the Count, she lived with Franz Liszt (q.v.) for several years and they had three children together. Some of the characters in Balzac's (q.v.) 1839 novel *Béatrix* were based on real people with d'Agoult as Béatrix de Rochefide.

D'Annunzio, Gabriele (1863–1938) an Italian poet who has been described as an early fascist and the inspiration for the future Italian dictator Benito Mussolini.

Daniel, a Jewish noble from Jerusalem who is the subject of the Bible's eponymous book. He is saved from lions because of his innocence: "My God hath sent his angel, and hath shut the lions' mouths, that they have not hurt me: forasmuch as before him innocency was found in me; and also before thee, O king, have I done no hurt."

Davidson, John (1857–1909) a Scottish poet and playwright. He influenced several Modernist poets. He died by suicide after suffering ill health and money troubles.

Davray (Henry Durand-Davray, 1873–1944) a French translator. He translated several of Wilde's poems into French. He also translated, together with Madeleine Vernon (q.v.), Frank

Harris's (q.v.) *Oscar Wilde: His Life and Confessions* into French.

de Chimay, Princesse (Clara Ward, 1873-1916) an American woman who had married a Belgian prince. She left her husband for a Hungarian musician, Rigó Jancsi (q.v.), who had been a Gypsy violinist at the restaurant where the Prince and Princess had been dining.

de Gourmont, Remy (1858-1915) a French poet and novelist. When asked what external influences he thought important in French literature replied: "Browning and Pater but, above all, Poe, Poe, through his son, Mallarmé" (q.v. all names).

de Guérin, Eugénie (1805-48) a French poet. Her brother, Maurice de Guérin, was the subject of an essay by Matthew Arnold (q.v.). She was very religious and a faithful Catholic.

de Musset, Alfred (1810-57) a French poet and novelist. He was in a relationship with George Sand (q.v.) from 1833 to 1835.

de Nerval, Gérard (Gérard Labrunie, 1808-55) a French poet, novelist and translator. He is remembered for having a pet lobster that he used to lead by a silk ribbon in the Palais-Royal in Paris. He suffered a number of nervous breakdowns, became interested in socialism and eventually took his own life.

De Quincey, Thomas (1785-1859) an English writer best remembered for his 1821 autobiographical *Confessions of an English Opium-Eater*. He also wrote a frank account of Samuel Taylor Coleridge (q.v.).

de Régnier, Henri (1864-1936) a French poet who came under the influence of symbolism. He was elected to the Académie Française in 1911.

de Rubempré, Lucien, a fictional character from Balzac's (q.v.) *Splendeurs et misères des courtisanes* who, while imprisoned, kills himself.

de Sales, St. Francis (1567-1622) a saintly Bishop of Geneva who was made a saint in 1665. He was then promoted to Doctor of the Church in 1877. In an 1932 encyclical, Pope Pius XI described him as "[one of] those brilliant examples of Christian perfection and wisdom … , he seemed to have been sent especially by God to contend against the heresies begotten by the Reformation."

de Staël, Madame (1766-1817, Anne Louise Germaine de Staël-Holstein) a French political activist. She predicted Napoleon's (q.v.) despotism and had to seek exile.

de Tinan, Jean (1874-98) a French novelist and part of the decadent movement. He had heart problems and drank a mixture of ether and curaçao to help with his pain. He died as a result of his illness at a young age.

Debussy, Claude (1862-1918) a French composer. He composed several symphonic works and the also the opera, *Pelléas et Mélisande*, first performed in Paris in 1902. Its opening reviews were mixed: "the noise of a squeaky door or a piece of furniture being moved about, or a child crying in the distance".

Delarue-Mardrus, Lucie (1874-1945) a prolific French poet and novelist. She wrote *Les amours d'Oscar Wilde* published in 1929.

Dickens, Charles (1812-70) an English writer who was extremely popular both now and in his lifetime. He was admired by many well-known writers. His critics complained of his sentimentalism: Trollope (q.v.) styled him in *The Warden* (1855) as Mr Popular-Sentiment and Wilde

Biographical notes

wrote to a friend that "One must have a heart of stone to read the death of little Nell without laughing."

Disraeli, Benjamin (1804-81) a British politician who served as prime minister in 1868 and 1874-80.

Dostoevsky, Fyodor (1821-81) a Russian writer. As a reformist he fell foul of Tsar Nicholas I and was exiled with hard labour to Siberia.

Douglas, Lord Alfred (1870-1945) an English poet and writer. He was nicknamed Bosie by his mother. His poem *Two Loves* (1894) ends with the line "I am the Love that dare not speak its name" that was read in Wilde's trial. Douglas met Wilde in 1891 and they began an affair that lasted for several years. It has been speculated that following Douglas's elder brother Francis's death in 1894, and that Francis had been suspected as being in a relationship with Lord Rosebery (q.v.), that Douglas's father, the Marquess of Queensbury (q.v.), began his hounding of Wilde to "save" his son.

Dowson, Ernest (1867-1900) an English poet and novelist and part of the decadent movement. The book title *Gone with the Wind* (1936) comes from one of his poems. After both his parents died he went into a decline and his health became worse. In order to help him, his publisher, Leonard Smithers (q.v.), gave him an allowance towards translation work. However, Dowson eventually gave this up and died at a young age. Wilde wrote of him: "Poor wounded wonderful fellow that he was, a tragic reproduction of all tragic poetry, like a symbol, or a scene. I hope bay leaves will be laid on his tomb and rue and myrtle too for he knew what love was."

Dreyfus, Alfred (1859-1935) a French army officer who was involved in a scandal eventually called the "Dreyfus affair". Dreyfus was convicted to life imprisonment for treason in 1894 but after a while new evidence pointed to another officer being responsible. Émile Zola (q.v.) campaigned for Dreyfus to have a retrial and he was found to have been innocent and was freed.

Du Maurier, George (1834-96) a French cartoonist and novelist who moved to London in about 1850. He contributed many cartoons to the British satirical magazine *Punch* and wrote *Trilby*, which was a best-selling book published in 1895.

Dubarry, Madame (Jeanne Bécu, Comtesse du Barry, 1743-93) the "official" mistress of King Louis XV of France who was executed during the Terror of the French revolution. In *The Diamond Necklace* a book by Thomas Carlyle (1837) describing a scandal in 1785 involving Queen Marie Antoinette and a supposed fraud, Dubarry is described as "A foul worm; hatched by royal heat, on foul composts, into a flaunting butterfly; now dis-winged, and again a worm!"

Dumas, Alexandre fils (1824-95) a French novelist and playwright. He is best known for his 1848 novel *La Dame aux Camélias* which was adapted into the 1853 opera *La Traviata*. His father (*père*) was also and author and famous for *The Three Musketeers*.

Eliot, George (Mary Anne Evans, 1819-80) an English author of seven novels in a realist style set in provincial England. In her novel *Adam Bede*, Mrs. Poyser's speech is written phonetically to represent the local dialect.

Erlynnes, Mrs., a fictional character from Wilde's 1892 play *Lady*

Windermere's Fan, A Play About a Good Woman.

Fawkes, Guido (1570-1606) also known as Guy Fawkes was an English Catholic who was involved in the failed Gunpowder Plot conspiracy of 1605 to kill King James I by blowing up the House of Lords during its state opening when the monarch would be present. Fawkes was discovered in the cellars guarding 36 barrels of gunpowder.

Flaubert, Gustave (1821-80) A French author. Well known for *Madame Bovary*, which was his first novel published in 1857. His work was very influential on other French novelists. He was known for working hard at his writing and his search for "*le mot juste*".

France, Anatole (François-Anatole Thibault, 1844-1924) a French author. Highly regarded in his time he was a member of the Académie Française, and was awarded the Nobel Prize in Literature in 1921.

Gambetta, Léon (1838-82) a French statesman and staunch defender of the French Republic. In 1888 a monument to Gambetta was placed in the Cour Napoléon, which was removed in the 1950s, and where the Louvre Pyramid by I.M. Pei is now located.

Gautier, Théophile (1811-72) a French poet and literary critic. Wilde's *The Picture of Dorian Gray* has Gray reading two of Gautier's poems.

Gide, André (1869-1951) a French author. He was awarded the Nobel Prize for literature in 1947 and his works were added to the Catholic Church's *Index Librorum Prohibitorum* (*List of Prohibited Books*) in 1952.

Gilbert, W. S. (1836-1911) an English librettist, dramatist and illustrator. He is perhaps best known for his collaboration with composer Arthur Sullivan and their resulting operettas. *Patience; or, Bunthorne's Bride*, first performed 1881, was a satire on the aesthetic movement and it is suggested that one of the characters was based on Wilde.

Gissing, George (1857-1903) an English novelist. In 1948, George Orwell said "Gissing's novels are a protest against the form of self-torture that goes by the name of respectability."

Goethe, Johann Wolfgang von (1749-1832) a German polymath. He met Napoleon (q.v.), the French monarch/dictator, in 1808 Napoleon was reported to have said: "*Vous êtes un homme!*" Together they discussed politics, the writings of Voltaire and Goethe's semi-autobiographical *Sorrows of Young Werther* (1774), which Napoleon had enjoyed very much.

Gogol, Nikolai (1809-52) a Ukrainian novelist and playwright well-known for absurdism and surrealism.

Goldsmith, Oliver (1728-74) an Irish novelist, playwright and poet. He is perhaps best known for *The Vicar of Wakefield* (1766).

Goncourt, Jules de (1830-70) and Edmond de (1822-96) were French writers and inseparable brothers. They collaborated on all their works.

Grolleau, Charles (1867-1940) a French writer and translator. He privately published *The Trial of Oscar Wilde* in 1906, which although being described as being based on shorthand reports is a much-shortened version of the court proceedings.

Grouchy, Emmanuel de (1766-1847) a French general in Napoleon's (q.v.) army. The reference to the text related to the Battle of Waterloo on 18 June 1815 where he pursued a part of a retreating Prussian army on 17 June,

Biographical notes

leaving Napoleon to be overwhelmed by the combined British and Prussian forces the next day.

Hall Caine, Thomas (1853–1931) an English novelist. He was secretary and companion to Gabriel Rossetti (q.v.) during the poet's final years. He published *Recollections of Rossetti* in 1882. Bram Stoker's 1897 *Dracula* includes a dedication to Hall Caine using his Stoker's joke name for him: "to my dear friend Hommy Beg".

Hardy, Thomas (1840–1928) an English novelist and poet. Many of his novels are set in the English countryside and end tragically.

Harland, Henry (1861–1905) an American novelist and editor. He was the founding editor of *The Yellow Book*, the quarterly literary magazine published between 1894 and 1897. The magazine never published any of Wilde's work. Aubrey Beardsley (q.v.) was the art editor and was dismissed by the publisher shortly after Wilde's arrest in 1895.

Harris, Frank (1855–1931) an Irish novelist and journalist who ran away to the USA at the age of thirteen. He studied the law but travelled to England and became a journalist. While Harris was the editor of the *Fortnightly Review* he came to know Wilde and they became friends. Harris published a biography of Wilde, *Oscar Wilde: His Life and Confessions*, in 1916. This appears to have been translated in to French by Davray and Vernon (both q.v.).

Hawthorne, Julian (1846–1934) an American writer and journalist. Son of the well-known Nathaniel (q.v.).

Hawthorne, Nathaniel (1804–64) an American novelist and short-story writer. Most famous for *The Scarlett Letter* of 1850.

Healy, Timothy (1855–1931) an Irish politician. He worked for nationalist politician Charles Parnell (q.v.). Healy eventually became the first Governor-General of the Irish Free State in 1922.

Heenan, John C. (1834–73) an American bare-knuckle boxer. He only had three formal fights; two ended in a draw and one lost. He married the actress Adah Isaacs Menken (q.v.) in 1859. According to Menken's biography Heenan mistreated her.

Henley, W. E. (1849–1903) an English poet and editor. At one stage he edited the *Scots Observer* and used this journal to criticize Wilde's poetry (specifically *The Ballad of Reading Gaol*) and *The Picture of Dorian Gray*. Henley suffered from poor health and had one leg amputated in his teenage years.

Hobbes, John Oliver *see* Craigie, Pearl.

Horton, William Thomas (1864–1919) an English illustrator. The book that the text refers to is *The Raven, The Pit and The Pendulum* by Edgar Allan Poe (q.v.), published by Leonard Smithers (q.v.) in 1899 with seven illustrations and a cover design by Horton and "some account of the author" by O'Sullivan.

Howells, W. D. (1837–1920) an American novelist and critic who was the editor of *The Atlantic Monthly* from 1871 to 1881.

Hugo, Victor (1802–85) a French novelist and playwright. He had a long career and is best known for his novels *The Hunchback of Notre-Dame* (1831) and *Les Misérables* (1862).

Hunt, Violet (1862–1942) an English writer. Her book, *The Wife of Rossetti* (1932) was a biography of Elizabeth Siddal (1829–62) who was the model and wife to Gabriel Rossetti (q.v.). It is thought that post-natal depression led to Siddal taking her own life by an overdose of laudanum.

Huysmans, Joris-Karl (Charles-Marie-Georges Huysmans 1848-1907) a French novelist most famous for *À Rebours* (*Against Nature*, 1884), a key text of the Decadent movement.

Ibsen, Henrik (1828-1906) a Norwegian playwright. His play *A Doll's House* (1879) is one of the world's most performed.

Illingworth Lord a character in Wilde's *A Woman of No Importance* (1892).

Irving, Henry (1838-1905) an English actor and theatre manager. Bram Stoker worked for Irving at one stage and it is suggested that the character Dracula is based on Irving.

Isabel (perhaps Isabella of Angoulême, 1186-1246) a French-born Queen of England. The text makes the connection with Jezebel (q.v.). Isabel and Jezebel (q.v.) are the same word in Hebrew and also, perhaps, refers to the Medieval chronicler, Matthew Paris (*c.*1200-59) who said of Isabella, the queen of King John, that she was "more Jezebel than Isabel".

James, Henry (1843-1916) an American author. He spent most of his adult life in Europe, mostly England. Wilde said of his work: "Mr. Henry James writes fiction as if it were a painful duty, and wastes upon mean motives and imperceptible 'points of view' his neat literary style, his felicitous phrases, his swift and caustic satire."

Jehu (reigned *c.*841-14BC) a king of Israel. He murdered his predecessor and also killed Jezebel (q.v.). Jezebel knowing of Jehu's arrival at her palace in Jezreel, dressed in fine clothes and a wig and taunted him. Some sources suggest that this was an attempt to look older and more commanding, not alluring. Jehu killed her by having her thrown from a palace window.

Jezebel (died *c.*842BC) a wife of one of the kings of Israel. As a biblical figure she is associated with false prophets. In popular culture she is a stereotype of a sexually adventurous and promiscuous woman. Jehu (q.v.) had her murdered.

John the Baptist (died *c.*30AD) a Jewish preacher. He criticized Herod, the ruler of Galilee, for divorcing his wife and then marrying Herodias, his brother's wife. During Herod's birthday celebration Salome, Herodias' daughter, danced for Herod and "he promised with an oath to give her whatsoever she would ask. And she, being before instructed of her mother, said, Give me here John Baptist's head in [on] a charger [platter]".

Johnson, Samuel Dr. (1709-84) an English writer and critic. The text refers to "Clarissa Harlowe" who is the fictional subject of Samuel Richardson's 1748 novel *Clarissa; or, The History of a Young Lady*. Johnson was recorded in his biography (by James Boswell) as replying to the comment "Surely, Sir, Richardson is very tedious" (the book was over 1500 pages) to which Johnson replied: "Why, Sir, if you were to read Richardson for the story, your impatience would be so much fretted that you would hang yourself. But you must read him for the sentiment, and consider the story as only giving occasion to the sentiment."

Johnson, Lionel (1867-1902) an English poet. He is said to have introduced Alfred Douglas (q.v.), who was his cousin, to Wilde. Johnson later regretted this when their affair became scandalous and wrote the

Biographical notes

sonnet "The Destroyer of a Soul" (1892) referred to in the text.

Jones, Henry Arthur (1851–1929) an English dramatist. Apparently, Jones did not particularly care for Wilde but he like to quote Wilde's observation: "There are three rules for writing plays. The first rule is not to write like Henry Arthur Jones; the second and third rules are the same."

Jonson, Ben (1572–1637) an English playwright and poet. He was a contemporary of Shakespeare (q.v.) and was supposedly a rival.

Joseph (died *c.*1445BC) a biblical figure who was sold by his brothers – jealous of his coat – as a slave but who became powerful figure in Egypt. The Egyptian Pharaoh allowed Joseph to bring his father, Jacob, and the rest of the family to Egypt. Years later, Moses was to lead Jacob's descendants out of slavery in Egypt to their promised land.

Kalergis, Maria (Maria Kalergis von Nesselrode-Ereshoven, 1822–74) a Polish patron of the arts. Richard Wagner (q.v.) was part of her salon and he dedicated *Das Judenthum in der Musik* ('Jewishness in Music', 1850) an attack on Jewish musicians, to her. A footnote to a modern edition mentions that she rescued Wagner from bankruptcy when he was in Paris in 1860. Whether the old anti-Semite knew of Kalergis' Jewish grandmother is not clear.

Keats, John (1795–1821) an English poet who was a prominent figure in English Romantic poetry.

Kipling, Rudyard (1865–1936) an English writer. During his lifetime he was a very popular author but he always divided opinion with critics. George Orwell, writing in 1941, said: "What is much more distasteful in Kipling than sentimental plots or vulgar tricks of style, is the imperialism to which he chose to lend his genius."

Knox, John (1514–72) a Scottish priest. He was a Protestant Reformer and his *The First Blast of the Trumpet Against the Monstruous Regiment of Women* (1558) was an attack on female monarchs.

La Jeunesse, Ernest (1874–1917) a French writer, journalist and illustrator. He contributed a section to what was translated as *In Memoriam Oscar Wilde* (1905) *Recollections of Oscar Wilde* (1906) and also as *The Truth About Oscar Wilde* (1906).

Lamb, Charles (1775–1834) an English writer and poet. His biographer described him as "the most loveable figure in English literature".

Lamennais, Hugues Felicité Robert de (1782–1854) a French Catholic priest who proposed political liberalism and social Catholicism.

Landor, Walter Savage (1775–1864) an English poet and writer who had strong ideas on political reform. One of his most well-known works is *Imaginary Conversations* (1822) from which Wilde quotes in *The Critic as Artist* (1891).

Lane, John (1854–1925) an English publisher who was a founder of The Bodley Head in 1887, which published the *The Yellow Book* from 1894 to 1897.

Lang, Andrew (1844–1912) a Scottish writer and academic who is best known for his books on folklore, mythology and religion. Lang was a Fellow of Oxford University and knew Wilde there when he was an undergraduate.

Langtry, Lily (1853–1929) a Jersey-born actress and socialite. She was mistress to the Prince of Wales (later King Edward VII) at one time.

Leclerq, Julien (1865-1901) a French poet and art critic. One of the exhibitions he organized was in Paris in March 1901 where he put together a retrospective of the work of Vincent van Gogh (q.v.) which helped to bring van Gogh's work to a wider audience. Leclerq died unexpectedly in October of that same year.

Lemonnier, Léon (1890-1953) a French writer and literary critic. He published *La vie d'Oscar Wilde* in 1931 (not 1932 as stated in the text).

Liszt, Franz (1811-86) a Hungarian composer and pianist who was very successful and well known during his lifetime. His daughter Cosmo became Richard Wagner's (q.v.) second wife.

Lloyd, Marie (1870-1922) an English music-hall actress. She was well known for her risqué songs.

Longfellow, Henry Wadsworth (1807-82) an American poet. During a tour of Britain he had tea with Queen Victoria (q.v.) who remarked later to her husband's biographer: "I noticed an unusual interest among the attendants and servants. I could scarcely credit that they so generally understood who he was. When he took leave, they concealed themselves in places from which they could get a good look at him as he passed. I have since inquired among them, and am surprised and pleased to find that many of his poems are familiar to them. No other distinguished person has come here that has excited so peculiar an interest. Such poets wear a crown that is imperishable."

Lorrain, Jean (Paul Alexandre Martin Duval, 1855-1906) a French poet and novelist. He was dandy and frequented the cafés and bars on Montmartre in Paris. He did not conceal his homosexuality and called himself "the Ambassador from Sodom".

Louÿs, Pierre (Pierre Félix Louis, 1870-1925) a Belgian poet and writer who moved to France. He is best known for his erotic writing. Louÿs knew Wilde well and was the subject of the dedication to the French version of *Salomé* ("À mon Ami Pierre Louÿs").

Lytton *see* **Bulwer-Lytton.**

Maeterlinck, Maurice (1862-1949) a Belgian playwright and poet. Although he was born in the Flemish-speaking region, he worked in the French language. He was awarded the Nobel Prize for literature in 1911.

Mallarmé, Stéphane (Étienne Mallarmé, 1842-98) a French poet. His work was the inspiration for musical compositions such as Claude Debussy's (q.v.) *Prélude à l'après-midi d'un faune* (1894).

Maturin, Charles (1780-1824) an Irish clergyman and writer best known for his 1820 novel *Melmoth the Wanderer*. Maturin was Wilde's mother's uncle. Wilde used the alias "Sebastian Melmoth" while in Paris. He also published a collection of aphorisms in 1904 under the title *Sebastian Melmoth*.

Maupassant, Guy de (1850-93) a French author. He was well known for his short stories and novel *Bel-Ami* (1885).

May, Phil (1864-1903) an English cartoonist.

Melmoth, Sebastian, a fictional character *see* Maturin, Charles.

Mendès, Catulle (1841-1909) a French poet and playwright. Despite what the text says he appears to have been a friend or at least a friendly acquaintance of Wilde's.

Biographical notes

Menken, Adah Isaacs (1835–68) an American actress. She was well known for a role in the equestrian drama *Mazeppa*. This probably explains why the text describes her as a circus-rider. Her third husband was John Heenan (q.v.), a boxer.

Meredith, George (1828–1909) an English poet and novelist. The line "They eat their pot of honey on a grave" (it should be "eat *our* pot of honey") is from *Modern Love* (1862) which tells of a collapsing marriage.

Merrill, Stuart (1863–1915) an American poet who wrote mainly in French. He was a friend of Wilde's and described how Wilde would "willingly profess himself an anarchist between two glasses of champagne".

Méryon, Charles (1821–68) a French artist. His colour-blindness meant he work mostly at etching.

Metternich, Pauline von (1836–1921) an Austrian socialite based in Vienna and Paris. She promoted the work of musicians such as Richard Wagner (q.v.) and Bedřich Smetana.

Meynell, Alice (1847–1922) an English writer. The "Palace Court" referred to in the text was her home at 47 Palace Court, Bayswater, London that she shared with her husband. When describing Aubrey Beardsley (q.v.) as having "a line in his hand", she could perhaps be thinking about palmistry, which was popular at the time. For example, having the "Girdle of Venus" on one's hand indicates "a tendency to debauchery, which it is extremely difficult to conquer".

Milton, John (1608–67) an English civil servant and poet most famous for *Paradise Lost* (1667).

Mirbeau, Octave (1848–1917) a French writer. One of his books, *Le Jardin des supplices* (translated as *The Torture Garden*, 1899) Wilde described as "revolting – a sort of grey adder". Mirbeau was a friend of Wilde's and defended him in the French press after his indecency trial.

Moore, George (1852–1933) an Irish writer. He published *Evelyn Innes* in 1898. Wilde and his older brother Willie knew Moore when they were children together. It is not clear why they fell out but Moore did seem to be able to make enemies of a large number of people easily. W.B. Yeats (q.v.) described him as "a man carved out of a turnip, looking out of astonished eyes".

Moore, Thomas (1779–1852) an Irish writer and poet who was a Catholic patriot and defended the Church against reformers. He was a friend of Lord Byron (q.v.) and along with John Hobhouse and Byron's publisher he burned Byron's "life and adventures" after his death in 1824.

Morand, Paul (1888–1976) a French author. He came from a wealthy family and was a Nazi collaborator during the Second World War. In 1968, after several attempts, he was admitted to the Académie Française, much to the annoyance of President de Gaulle, France's wartime leader.

Morris, William (1834–96) an English designer and writer. He was a friend and worked together with Gabriel Rossetti (q.v.). His nickname "Topsy" supposedly comes from the name of a character in *Uncle Tom's Cabin* (1852). He came from a wealthy family, dabbled with socialism and Marxism, and like many of this type of person he was parsimonious with his own money.

Napoleon (Napoléon Bonaparte, 1769–1821) a French monarch/dictator whose attempt to control the whole of Europe ended in defeat at the Battle of Waterloo in 1815. He divorced his first wife, Joséphine (1763–1814) after she was unable to produce an heir and married Marie Louise (1791–1847) who gave birth to the "King of Rome" in 1811. The Napoleon cocktail mentioned in the text appears to have several recipes today with gin, orange liqueur and Dubonnet being the most popular ingredients.

Napoleon III (Charles Louis Napoléon Bonaparte, 1808–73) president of France (1848–52) and then emperor (1852–70). He oversaw the Haussmann renovation of Paris (1852–70).

Nero (Nero Claudius Caesar Augustus Germanicus, 37–68) a Roman emperor. Tactitus in his *Annals* (69–116) describes Nero using Christians as scapegoats for the fire that raged in Rome at the time.

Newman, Cardinal (John Henry Newman, 1801–90) an English cardinal of the Catholic Church. The text includes a quotation from *The Idea of a University* (1852): "Hence it is that it is almost a definition of a gentleman to say he is one who never inflicts pain. ... He has too much good sense to be affronted at insults, he is too well employed to remember injuries, and too indolent to bear malice."

Nichols, Harry Sidney (1865–1941) an English publisher. He was a business partner of Leonard Smithers (q.v.) and was mainly involved in publishing pornography and had to leave England to avoid prosecution, first to Paris (1900–8) and then to the USA (from 1908).

Nicole, Pierre (1625–95) a French barrister who was a leading figure in the Jansenist sect of the Catholic Church.

Nietzsche, Friedrich (1844–1900) A German philosopher. The "blond beast" referenced in the text is a metaphor used in *On the Genealogy of Morality: A Polemic* (1887). He posits that the "blonde [sic] beast ... lies at the core of all aristocratic races" and presciently mentions "The profound, icy mistrust which the German provokes, as soon as he arrives at power ... of that inextinguishable horror with which for whole centuries Europe has regarded the wrath of the blonde Teuton beast."

O'Connell, Daniel (1775–1847) an Irish political leader who worked to bring Catholic emancipation to Ireland. Balzac (q.v.) called him "the incarnation of a people" and described him along with Napoleon (q.v.) as one of the greatest men of the nineteenth century.

Octavius, Gaius (Caesar Augustus, 63BC–AD14) first Roman emperor. "His ears were of moderate size, and his nose projected a little at the top and then bent slightly inward."

Offenbach, Jacques (1819–80) a German composer who worked in France. He composed many operettas including *The Tales of Hoffmann*.

Orange, William of (1650–1702) King William III of England, Scotland and Ireland from 1689 to his death. Unhappy with King James and his Catholic leanings, some politicians and religious leaders arranged for the staunchly Protestant William to stage an invasion – called the Glorious Revolution – from the Netherlands to depose James. While England and Scotland welcomed the new king, Catholic Ireland did not and William invaded and eventually defeated Jacobite forces at the Battle of the Boyne in 1690. One soldier from the Netherlands who fought with William was Colonel de Wilde, an ancestor of Wilde's.

Biographical notes

Ouida (Marie Louise de la Ramée, 1839-1908) an English novelist who mostly wrote adventure stories.

Parnell, Charles (1846-91) an Irish politician who was a member of the Home Rule League campaigning for Ireland to have its own government within the UK.

Pater, Walter (1839-94) an English literary critic and writer. In *The Picture of Dorian Gray*, one character quotes from Pater's *Marius the Epicurean: His sensations and ideas* (1885). Pater felt that Wilde's depiction of epicureanism was flawed: "A true Epicureanism aims at a complete though harmonious development of man's entire organism. To lose the moral sense therefore, for instance the sense of sin and righteousness, as Mr. Wilde's heroes are bent on doing so speedily, as completely as they can, is … to become less complex, to pass from a higher to a lower degree of development."

Peter and Paul, saints of the Christian Church who were blamed for the Great Fire of Rome (AD64) and were martyred by Nero (q.v.).

Pinero, Arthur Wing (1855-1934) an English actor and playwright. His works have not survived the test of time.

Pitt, William (1759-1806) an English politician. He was Britain's youngest prime minister (he was often called "the younger" to distinguish him from his father "William Pitt the Elder"). It was during Pitt's tenure that he had to contend with the American War of Independence and the Napoleonic Wars.

Plato (427-247BC) an Ancient Greek philosopher. He was a student of Socrates and together they are major figures in western philosophy and religion. Wilde uses a Socratic dialogue in his essay "The Decay of Lying" (1891) in a manner similar to the allegory of the cave from Plato's *Republic* (c.375BC) to argue against realism and for romanticism.

Poe, Edgar Allan (1809-49) an American writer particularly well known for his mystery and macabre works. His early life was traumatic with his father abandoning the family in 1810 and his mother dying in 1811. He had a problematic relationship with alcohol throughout his life and many people speculate that this was the cause of his premature death.

Pope, Alexander (1688-1744) an English poet. He was one of the most quoted eighteenth-century sources in the *Oxford English Dictionary*. His most famous poem was *The Rape of the Lock* (1712).

Poulet-Malassis, Auguste (1825-78) a French publisher who was a friend of Baudelaire (q.v.) and published many of his works; he was prosecuted for issuing one of Baudelaire's banned works.

Pourtalès, Mélanie de (Countess Edmond de Pourtalès, 1836-1914) a French socialite based in Paris.

Proust, Marcel (1871-1922) a French novelist famous for his multi-part *À la recherche du temps perdu* (1913-27). In this work, one of the characters translated Ruskin's (q.v.) *Sesame and Lilies* (1865) and Proust was said to know *The Bible of Amiens* (1884) by heart.

Prout, Father (Francis Sylvester Mahony, 1804-66) an Irish writer who wrote witty pieces.

Quaritch, Bernard (1819-99) a German-born bookseller who worked in London.

Queensberry, Marquess of (John Sholto Douglas, 1844-1900) a Scottish aristocrat. He did not like the fact that his son Lord Alfred Douglas (q.v.) was in a relationship with Wilde and he left a calling card at the Albemarle Club for Wilde describing him as a "posing somdomite [sic]". This caused Wilde to sue for libel but the case collapsed and Wilde was forced to pay costs which ruined him. Shortly after the case, Wilde was arrested and prosecuted for gross indecency.

Quintilian (Marcus Fabius Quintilianus, c.35–100AD) a Roman rhetorician. The text quotes from *Institutio Oratoria* and is perhaps translated as "But modesty and circumspection are required in pronouncing judgment on such great men".

Racine, Jean (1639–99) a French playwright and important figure in western drama.

Ravachol (François Claudius Koenigstein, 1859–92) a French anarchist who was executed by guillotine for murder.

Reade, Charles (1814–84) an English novelist chiefly remembered for *The Cloister and the Hearth* (1861) which is a novel set in the fifteenth century about a scribe's struggle between family and the Church. Wilde, in his essay "The Decay of Lying" (1891) describes the novel as a "beautiful book" but berates Reade as having "wasted the rest of his life in a foolish attempt to be modern".

Réjane, Gabrielle (1856–1920) a French actress. She performed in several European cities and was very popular in London between 1877 and 1915.

Rigó, Jancsi (1858–1927) a Hungarian Gypsy violinist. He eloped with Princesse de Chimay (q.v.). The scandal led an enterprising pastry chef to produce a chocolate sponge cake called Rigójancsi which is still popular today.

Ritter, Franziska (1829–95) a German actress. She was the niece of Richard Wagner (q.v.) and married to composer Alexander Ritter. The couple were familiar with many leading musicians and Alexander was supposed to have encouraged Richard Strauss (q.v.) to move from his conservative style to tone poems. Strauss went on to compose *Salome* (1905) a one-act opera based on Wilde's 1891 play *Salomé*.

Robertson, Fanny (Mary Frances Ross, 1765–1855) an English actor and theatre manager. Mainly based in theatres in Lincolnshire.

Rops, Félicien (1833–98) a Belgian artist and engraver. Critics varied in their opinions: some described his work as pornographic and Baudelaire (q.v.) considered him the greatest Belgian artist of his time.

Rosebery, Lord (Archibald Philip Primrose, 1847–1929) an English politician who was prime minister from 1894 to 1895. It is thought that he had a relationship with Francis Douglas [Alfred Douglas's (q.v.) eldest brother] and that an enraged Marquess of Queensbury (q.v.) threatened to expose the affair if Rosebery interfered with Wilde's prosecution regarding Alfred. Francis died from the result of injuries during a shooting party. However, there were rumours that the death was suicide or even murder.

Ross, Robbie (Robert Ross, 1869–1918) a Canadian journalist and art critic. He is thought to have been Wilde's first male lover and was a loyal friend to Wilde. He also acted as Wilde's literary executor.

Rossetti, Christina (1830–94) an English poet. She was the sister of

Biographical notes

Gabriel Rossetti (q.v.) and William Michael Rossetti (q.v.).

Rossetti, Gabriel (Dante Gabriel Rossetti, 1828–82) an English poet, painter and illustrator who founded the Pre-Raphaelite Brotherhood of painters and poets. He was the eldest brother of Christina Rosetti (q.v.) and William Michael Rossetti (q.v.) and husband to Elizabeth Siddall (see the entry for Violet Hunt).

Rossetti, William Michael (1829–1919) an English writer. He acted as the unofficial organizer and bibliographer to the Pre-Raphaelite Brotherhood of painters and poets. He edited the literary works of his brother Gabriel Rossetti (q.v.) and sister Christina Rossetti (q.v.).

Rostand, Maurice (1891–1968) a French author and playwright.

Ruskin, John (1819–1900) an English art critic and social reformer. Marcel Proust (q.v.) admired his works and translated them into French. The text mentions Ruskin's "sentimentalizing" of workmen and this was realized in 1874–5 when as a professor of fine art at Oxford University, he and a group of undergraduates repaired a road outside of the city. A memorial plaque still stands mentioning that the effort was to improve the road and "feel the pleasure of useful muscular work". Incredibly, the group was said to have included Wilde. The views of the sentimentalized labourers deprived of their wages do not appear to have been recorded.

Saint Augustine (Aurelius Augustinus Hipponensis, 354–430) a Christian theologian and bishop of Roman north Africa. Augustine's *Confessions*, written between 397 and 400, was one of his most enduring works where he describes his sinful early life (in Book 2, as a teenager, he admits to the theft of a pear) and eventual conversion of Christianity. The Latin quotation in the text (*Inquietum est cor nostrum, donec requiescat in te*) is from *Confessions* and is roughly translated as "Our heart is restless until it rests in you".

Saint Teresa *see* Teresa of Ávila.

Sainte-Beuve, Charles (1804–69) a French literary critic. He was nominated to the chair of Latin poetry at the College of France in Paris by Napoleon III. When giving his lectures he was so frequently interrupted by disapproving students that he decided to resign his position.

Saltus, Edgar (1855–1921) an American writer of the decadent style. The book obliquely referred to in the text was *The Truth About Tristrem Varick* (1888).

Sand, George (Amantine Lucile Aurore Dupin, 1804–76) a French novelist of the Romantic style. She was an unconventional woman of her time, frequently wearing men's clothing. Sand had affairs with Chopin (q.v.) and de Musset (q.v.).

Sardou, Victorien (1831–1908) a French playwright. Several of his plays were transformed into operas, including *Tosca*. Eggs Sardou, a Creole dish, was named after him following a visit to New Orleans.

Schubert, Franz (1797–1828) an Austrian composer of the Romantic era. He was prolific and his music increased in popularity after his early death.

Schumann, Robert (1810–86) a German composer of the Romantic era. After an attempted suicide he was admitted to an asylum where he died from pneumonia.

Schuster, Mariana Emily (1833–1919) the daughter of Leo Schuster who was born in Germany and moved to England aged about seventeen. After several successful business ventures he went on to form a merchant bank, Schuster Sons & Co., in the City of London.

Schwob, Marcel (1867-1905) a French novelist who was well-known for his short stories. He had an enormous number of friends in the arts and literature community. Schwob proofread and corrected Wilde's French for his play *Salomé*.

Scott, Clement (1841-1904) an English theatre critic for the *Daily Telegraph* newspaper. His reviews were often overly critical and after one such article there was such an outcry that he was forced to retire. He married Isabel du Maurier, the sister of George du Maurier (q.v.).

Scribe, Eugène (1791-1861) a French playwright known also as a librettist. He wrote in the *la pièce bien faite* ("well-made play") style that involves an intricate plot, sometimes based on events that took place prior to the events in the play, suspense building up to a climax where all is resolved.

Shakespeare, William (1564-1616) one of England's most famous playwrights. In the text, Wilde responds to O'Sullivan's comment about there being too many "people of title" in his plays. In answer, Wilde refers to Shakespeare and, indeed, people have also queried Shakespeare's overuse of aristocrats. In 1914, "Is Shakespeare Aristocratic?" comments: "We are led to wonder whether the contempt expressed in [*Julius Caesar*] for the vile-smelling and fickle-minded Roman mob represents Shakespeare's own attitude toward his humbler fellow-citizens." This type of reasoning and lack of empathy for the time in which Shakespeare's works were written is part of the whole question that persists today of certain "celebrities" questioning if Shakespeare was too ordinary or common to write his own plays. Academics and scholars are dismissive of this theory.

Sheridan, Richard Brinsley (1751-1816) an Irish playwright. His plays were extremely successful in London and are still performed today. He was a Member of Parliament for 32 years.

Sitwell, Edith (1887-1964) an English poet and writer. The book referred to in the text, *Life of Alexander Pope* (q.v.), is titled *Alexander Pope* and was first published in 1930.

Smithers, Alice (Alice Edith Oldham, c.1867-?) married Leonard Smithers (q.v.) in 1882 as his second wife. She is described variously as "plain but ever good-tempered", "a broad good-natured ex-trollop" and, in this text, as "full-bodied, high-coloured, with snapping black eyes and hair to match, and—yes, pretty" and "Black hair, black eyes, smiling, florid, buxom and healthy, with full shoulders, breasts and arms, she was ready to talk really quite pleasantly".

Smithers, Leonard (1861-1907) an English publisher who produced many of the decadent publications of the late 1800s (including many of Vincent O'Sullivan's books). He also published material considered by many to be pornographic and is supposed to have added a sign to his London bookshop stating "Smut is Cheap Today". He died a bankrupt.

Sorel, Julien, a character in Stendal's (pen name of Marie-Henri Beyle, 1783-1842) *The Red and the Black* (*Le Rouge et le Noir*, 1830). He was executed for attempted murder.

Soulary, Joséphin (1815-91) a French poet. He was admired during his lifetime and Charles Baudelaire (q.v.)

Biographical notes

wrote to him after receiving his new book that "I was able to relish its quite unique flavour, all its vinosity".

Steele, Richard (1672-1729) an Irish playwright. He was part of the Irish Protestant gentry and after education at Charterhouse School and Oxford University he joined the army and later became a Whig member of parliament.

Stevenson, Robert Louis (1850-94) a Scottish novelist. He was prolific and *Treasure Island* (1882) still influences the way many perceive pirates. The Pew character, "Blind Pew", is a violent and sinister beggar.

Strauss, Richard (1864-1949) a German composer. He wrote many works over a long period of time. One of his early very successful operas was *Salome*, first performed in 1905, that was based on Wilde's play *Salomé*.

Strindberg, August (1849-1912) a Swedish playwright who became famous internationally.

Strong, Rowland (1865-1924) an English journalist based in Paris, perhaps the correspondent of the *New York Times*.

Surtees, Robert Smith (1805-64) an English novelist. His work was perhaps not suited to the Victorian period of sentimental writing. Norman Gash, a modern historian writing in 2004 describes his work as follows: "His leading male characters were coarse or shady; his leading ladies dashing and far from virtuous; his outlook on society satiric to the point of cynicism."

Swift, Jonathan (1667-1745) an Irish writer. He was famous as a satirist. The relationships referred in the text appear to be with Esther Vanhomrigh (1688-1723) who he was with for seventeen years. She reacted angrily to his relationship with Esther Johnson (1681-1728). The bitterness may have led to Vanhomrigh's early death. Beforehand, she destroyed the will she had left in Swift's favour. Johnson in turn died at a relatively young age.

Swinburne, Algernon Charles (1837-1909) an English playwright of the decadent movement. His family was wealthy and he was educated as Eton College and Oxford University. His restless nervousness was perhaps responsible for his alcoholism and masochism which led to his eventual removal from society to live soberly in the care of Theodore Watts-Dunton (q.v.). Wilde said of Swinburne: "a braggart in matters of vice, who had done everything he could to convince his fellow citizens of his homosexuality and bestiality without being in the slightest degree a homosexual or a bestializer".

Swinburne, Lady Jane (Jane Henrietta, 1809-96) the fifth daughter of the Third Earl of Ashburnham and the mother of Algernon Charles Swinburne (q.v.).

Symons, Arthur (1865-1945) a Welsh poet. He contributed to *The Yellow Book* and edited with Leonard Smithers (q.v.) the *Savoy* magazine. He suffered from a mental illness in 1909 and this restricted his writing for about twenty years.

Tannhäuser (c.1245-65) a, perhaps legendary, German poet and minstrel. Now mostly associated with Wagner's (q.v.) 1845 opera of the same name.

Taylor, Tom (1817-80) an English playwright and later editor of *Punch* magazine. Ellen Terry (q.v.), the actress, remembered him: "Most people know that Tom Taylor was one of the leading playwrights of the 'sixties … but to us he was more than this. He was an institution! I simply cannot remember when I did not know him."

Tchekov, Anton Pavlovich (1860–1904) a Russian playwright and short story writer. His most notable plays include *The Seagull* (1896), *Uncle Vanya* (1897), *Three Sisters* (1901) and *The Cherry Orchard* (1904).

Teixera de Mattos, Alexander (1865–1921) a Dutch translator fluent in Danish, Dutch, English, French and German. In 1900 he married Lily Wilde, the widow of Wilde's older brother Willie (q.v.).

Tennyson, Alfred (Alfred, Lord Tennyson, 1809–92) an English poet. He was Queen Victoria's (q.v.) poet laureate. The line in the text: "Now lies the earth all Danae to the stars" is from "Now Sleeps the Crimson Petal" which is part of *The Princess* (1847). Danaë is a mortal character from Greek mythology. She was the mother of Perseus, the great hero, conceived from Zeus, king of the gods.

Teresa of Ávila (Teresa Sánchez de Cepeda y Ahumada, 1515–82) a saint of the Catholic Church. She was well known for her asceticism and meditative praying.

Terry, Ellen (1847–1928) an English actress. Paintings of her by her husband led to her become something of a cult figure for poets and painters in the aesthetic and Pre-Raphaelite movements.

Terry, Fred (1863–1933) an English actor and younger brother to Ellen and Marion Terry (both q.v.). He played the role of Gerald Arbuthnot in Wilde's play *A Woman of No Importance* in its first production in 1892.

Terry, Marion (1853–1930) an English actress. She played the role of Mrs Erlynne in Wilde's play *Lady Windermere's Fan* in 1892 to great acclaim. She was rather overshadowed by her sister Ellen Terry (q.v.). The text mentions the character of Gerald Arbuthnot in *A Woman of No Importance*: it seems unlikely Marion would have played that part and it is more likely Fred Terry (q.v.), her brother, to whom O'Sullivan refers.

Thackeray, William Makepeace (1811–63) an English novelist. He was born in India but was sent to England as a child following the death of his father. The Brookfields mentioned in the text were the family of Jane Brookfield (1821–96) a literary hostess, with whom Thackeray enjoyed a close friendship.

Thompson, Francis (1859–1907) an English poet. He trained as a doctor but gave this up to become a writer. After failing to earn a living he ended up living rough. He was taken up by Alice Meynell (q.v.) and together with her husband published Thompson's work.

Toulouse-Lautrec, Henri de (1864–1901) a French artist. He was a friend of Wilde's and painted a portrait of him in watercolour in 1895 on the night before his trial. The background of the painting shows a sketch of the Houses of Parliament in London. Whether this was to show Wilde turning his back on Britain or merely to locate the painting in London is open to speculation.

Traill, Henry Duff (1842–1900) an English writer. He wrote a few novels, many articles and pamphlets, and biographies. Although O'Sullivan describes him as "a writer of considerable repute", his reputation has not survived him.

Biographical notes

Trollope, Anthony (1815–82) an English novelist. He is famous for his Barsetshire novels.

Turner, J.M.W. (1775–1851) an English artist. He is famous for his innovative painting style. John Ruskin was a great supporter of Turner and described him as an artist who "stirringly and truthfully measure the moods of Nature".

Turveydrop, Mr. A fictional character from Charles Dickens's (q.v.) 1853 *Bleak House*. "Very gentlemanly indeed … He is celebrated almost everywhere for his deportment."

van Gogh, Vincent (1853–90) a Dutch painter recognized as one of the most influential painters some years after his death by suicide.

Verlaine, Paul (1844–96) a French poet associated with the decadent movement. He lived in poverty in his final years and became an alcoholic and drug abuser.

Vernon, Madeleine, a French translator and actor. She translated, together with Henry Davay (q.v.), Frank Harris's (q.v.) *Oscar Wilde: His Life and Confessions* into French.

Victoria, Queen (1819–1901) the long-reigning British monarch whose name came to define the Victorian era which was popularly considered moralistic and prudish.

Villiers de l'Isle-Adam (Jean-Marie-Mathias-Philippe-Auguste, comte de Villiers de l'Isle-Adam, 1838–89) a French writer. He was born in Brittany to an impoverished aristocratic family. *L'Ève future*, published in 1886, is a science-fiction novel and is thought to have popularized the word "android" as being a human-like robot.

Villon, François (c.1431–63) a French poet. He was involved in several criminal activities, the final known one led to his banishment from Paris after which he was not heard of again.

Virgil (Publius Vergilius Maro, 70–19BC) a Roman poet. Many years after his death and up until medieval times, some have thought that Virgil's works had magical properties and that the future could be divined.

Wagner, Richard (1813–83) a German composer known chiefly for his operas. Some consider that Wagner influenced Nazi philosophy. What is sure is that Wagner hated Jewish people and dabbled with racial theories.

Wales, Prince of (Albert Edward, 1841–1910) the future monarch King Edward VII. He was the heir apparent for 60 years to Queen Victoria (q.v.).

Walpole, Horace (1717–97) an English writer and politician. A contemporary described him "in that style of affected delicacy, which fashion had made almost natural, *chapeau bras* [three-cornered hat] between his hands as if he wished to compress it, or under his arm; knees bent, and feet on tip-toe, as if afraid of a wet floor. His summer dress of ceremony was usually a lavender suit, the waistcoat embroidered with a little silver, or of white silk …, partridge silk stockings, gold buckles, ruffles and lace frill". He was the member of parliament for Callington in Cornwall, a pocket borough (or better described as a rotten borough) for thirteen years, although he never visited his constituency.

Watteau, Antoine (1684–1721) a French artist credited with the notion of the artist as an individual independent of the demands of contemporary style.

Ward, Clara *see* de Chimay, Princesse.

Watts-Dunton, Theodore (1832-1914) an English poet. He cared for poet and recovering alcoholic Algernon Charles Swinburne (q.v.) at the end of his life.

Wesendonck, Mathilde (*née* Luckemeyer, 1828-1902) a German poet. She is thought to have been a lover of Richard Wagner (q.v.).

Wesendonck, Otto (1815-96) a German silk merchant and art patron. Together with his wife, Agnes Wesendonck, he befriended Richard Wagner (q.v.) and allowed Wagner to stay in a cottage on their estate.

Wesley, John (1703-91) an English preacher and a founder of the Methodist Church.

Whibley, Charles (1859-1930) an English author and journalist. He was the Paris correspondent for the *Pall Mall Gazette*, a paper that supported Conservative politics. He was married to Ethel Philip (1861-1920) whose sister, Beatrice (1857-96) was married to James McNeill Whistler (q.v.).

Whistler, James McNeill (1834-1903) an American artist who worked mostly in England. He was friendly with Wilde but they eventually fell out.

Whitman, Walt (1819-92) an American poet. He was a humanist and his work, particularly *Leaves of Grass* (1855) was controversial during his lifetime. Nowadays he is considered one of America's most important poets.

Wilde, Dolly (Dorothy, 1895-1941) an English socialite based in Paris. She was the only child of Willie Wilde (q.v.) and niece of Oscar Wilde. She had a long relationship with Natalie Clifford Barney (q.v.).

Wilde, Willie (William, 1852-99) an Irish journalist and elder brother of Oscar. He was an alcoholic and a poor manager of money and this probably led to his early death.

Wills, W. G. (William Gorman, 1828-91) an Irish playwright, novelist and painter. He was fairly successful in his lifetime but after his death his work was not particularly considered in good favour. One critic writing in 1932 thought Wills' work "wavered between uninspired verse plays and noisy melodrama".

Wordsworth, William (1770-1850) an English Romantic poet.

Wotton, Lord Henry ("Harry") a fictional character in *The Picture of Dorian Gray* (1891). He is a hedonistic dandy. The character is thought to be based on Lord Ronald Gower (1845-1916) a friend of Wilde's who was implicated in a scandal when a male brothel in Cleveland Street, London was raided in 1889.

Yeats, W. B. (William Butler, 1865-1939) an Irish poet and writer who was awarded the Nobel Prize for Literature in 1923.

Ysovskaya (perhaps Marija Orskaja, 1893-1930) an actress born in the Russian Empire. She played Salome several times in Hamburg and Berlin in the 1920s. Her addiction to opiates led to her early death. (Unable to find Ysovskaya or actresses similarly named.)

Zola, Émile (1840-1902) a French novelist well known for his naturalistic books. He also campaigned for Alfred Dreyfus (q.v.), a falsely accused French army officer.

www.ingramcontent.com/pod-product-compliance
Lightning Source LLC
Chambersburg PA
CBHW041307110526
44590CB00028B/4277